To MIKE

Merry Christmas 1997

The Furlongs.

KINGSTON PAST

First published 1997
by Historical Publications Ltd
32 Ellington Street, London N7 8PL
Tel: 0171-607 1628

ISBN 0 948667 45 1
British Library Cataloguing-in-Publication Data
A catalogue record of this book is available from the British Library

Typeset in Palatino by Historical Publications Ltd
Reproduction by G & J Graphics, EC2
Printed in Zaragoza, Spain by Edelvives

KINGSTON PAST

June Sampson

Acknowledgements

This book could not have been completed without support from many people, notably Kingston's Heritage Officer, Anne McCormack; Local History Officer, Tim Everson; Kingston Museum's Collections Curator, Paul Hill; Archivist, Jill Lamb; Conservation Officer, Martin Higgins; and local historian, Shaan Butters. Their patience and enthusiasm never faltered in the face of my incessant demands. I am also grateful to the people – too numerous to list here – who have given or lent me items for my local history collection over the last 25 years.

The Illustrations

With the exception of those noted below the illustrations were supplied by the Author. We should like to thank all those who lent pictures.

Jane Alexander: *26*
Barnardo's: *43, 44*
Bentalls: *164, 165, 166*
British Aerospace: *184, 185, 186*
Peter Drewett: *149*
Miss B. Finny: *1*
Molly Jones (sister of Amy Johnson): *186*
Kingston Museum and Heritage Service: *2, 5, 8, 11, 12, 18, 22, 23, 29, 59, 63, 68, 71, 72, 110, 111, 116, 138, 140, 144, 146, 168, 171*
Dorothy Lockett: *122*
Queens Royal Surrey Regimental Association: *82*
Salvation Army International Heritage Service: *36, 37*
Smiths Industries: *132*
Michael Turk: *48, 75, 77*
Christopher Wilson: *183*

1. *Kingston Bridge in 1823, and the major route into Kingston, along Portsmouth Road and West-by-Thames (later renamed High Street).*

The First Kingstonians

Heroes of English legend were striding around the Kingston area some 1,400 years ago, nobly embellished with swords and shields. Indeed, one of the most popular exhibits in Kingston Museum is the skeleton of such a warrior, with Saxon shield bosses and swords, dating from between the 6th and 7th centuries. But they were by no means the first on the scene. More than 200,000 years earlier, during the Paleolithic, or Old Stone Age, nomadic hunters roamed the area carrying flint hand axes.

During the Mesolithic, or Middle Stone Age, the barren landscape began to fill with trees and shrubs, and the range and quality of implements was improved. Men made axes with long shafts, to cleave through trees when clearing forest land for camp settlements; scrapers to strip skin and meat from their prey; and efficient flint knives, with a razor sharp finish.

The Kingston area then, some 7,000 years ago, was well forested, and the Thames flood plain offered a rich variety of waterfowl, mammals and fish. People lived in seasonal dwellings, rather like large wooden tents, and were constantly on the move, following the herds of deer, wild cattle and other hunted animals as they migrated. Men hunted in parties, staying away from camp for days at a time, while women reared the children and collected seeds, berries and fruit.

By the end of the Mesolithic period, an intricate stone tool technology had evolved, together with a detailed knowledge of the environment. Many flint tools from this period have been dredged from the Thames, or unearthed during digs in and around Kingston. These can be seen in Kingston Museum.

Dramatic changes occurred in the Neolithic Age, from about 4,500 BC. The hunting/gathering existence was replaced by a settled life of arable and livestock farming. Permanent homes replaced temporary camps; crops were cultivated, and grain was stored in pits. Pottery-making improved, which meant that food could be cooked more easily and menus greatly expanded. Many Neolithic stone and flint axes have been found in and around Kingston. They are ground and polished – an important technological development. Several can be traced to well-known axe factories in Cornwall and Cumbria, indicating how trade advanced during this period.

The Thames area around Kingston became one of Britain's major wharving and manufacturing centres during the Bronze Age, from about 1100 to 700 BC.

2. *Reconstruction of an Iron Age settlement c. 400 BC, unearthed in Percy Gardens, Old Malden.*

Bronzemaking required copper from the Continent, and tin from the west country. Thanks to the river, these could easily be routed to Kingston. A wealth of Bronze Age artefacts have been unearthed in and around Kingston of a quality said to be second to none in Europe.

This period saw the erosion of the previously classless society as the old concept of communal power clashed with the new one of individual strength. Thus it is likely that some people boasted jewellery, wrist guards and bronze daggers to indicate their power, while others clung to the old order. This new individuality is evident in Bronze Age pottery found in Kingston with patterns denoting the social status of the owner. Kingston Hill has yielded evidence of a major metal working factory of that period, together with a wealth of beautiful artefacts. Other finds include pots, some containing ashes and buried in pits, indicating a burial tradition. Others contained grain, which suggests agriculture; and the discovery of post holes, stake holes, and loom weights implies that 3,000 years ago people lived in wattle and daub houses, kept sheep, and wove wool in what is now Kingston's most prestigious residential area.

Experts at Kingston Museum believe there are religious and economic reasons why so many fine Bronze Age weapons have been found in the local stretch of the Thames. These, they say, are prestige goods that would have lost value if they became too common. Ritually twisting or breaking them, then sacrificing them to the river gods, was a way of controlling the market, and preventing over-supply.

The Iron Age (*c*.700 BC to the Roman invasion of AD 43) largely displaced the use of bronze, and the Kingston area lost much of its prosperity. Few remains of this era have been found in the town centre. But a major Iron Age site was unearthed near Manor Drive North, Old Malden in the 1940s. It was a farm settlement of daub and wattle huts with thatched roofs and beaten gravel floors, surrounded by an exterior bank and ditch. Old Malden yielded another major find in 1991 when a sizeable Iron Age village was unearthed in Percy Gardens. Another Iron Age settlement was discovered at Alpine Avenue, Tolworth in 1991. This contained storage pits, large quantities of pottery and a fragment of quern stone – used for crushing grain. Loom weights were also found, suggesting that wool was woven here.

THE ROMANS

There is an unproven theory that Julius Caesar brought his army across the Thames at Kingston when he invaded Britain for the second time in 54 BC. But he did not conquer the country. That was left to the

Emperor Claudius, who led an invasion in AD 43.

Did Romans settle in Kingston? Did they have much influence on the Britons already living there? Evidence was scanty until 1989, when excavations by the Museum of London in Eden Street revealed traces of sustained Roman activitiy in Kingston town centre. It was a large indentation, cut into the gravel in an L-shape, containing numerous sherds of Roman pottery, tiles and building materials suggestive of a high class Roman residence nearby, with underfloor heating, a luxurious kitchen and painted murals. The oldest finds dated from the first century, but the majority were from about AD 330 to 370, during the later stages of the Roman occupation. A specially endearing item was a handsome red floor tile, disfigured by the imprints of a hobnailed boot – probably left by a careless workman clumping across it before it had time to dry. Another tile bore the pawprint of a dog.

Close by, in an ancient silted water channel, was jewellery and 340 assorted Roman coins. Philip Emery, the director of the dig, thinks this may have been a crossing place over a shallow watercourse. It was a Roman custom to appease water deities by throwing coins from the bank before crossing a river or stream (a custom echoed today in the form of wishing wells). Those who had no cash would throw small pieces of jewellery instead. For example, there was a child's bracelet, daintily made from braided bronze wire, dating from about AD 250. There was also women's jewellery and a bronze fibula brooch, once used by a Roman to fasten his toga. A more sinister custom was recalled by a rolled-up strip of lead sheeting tossed into the water more than sixteen centuries ago. The Museum of London explain that people inscribed curses on lead, then threw them in the river. Lead was considered a good medium for curses since the metal was associated with the god Saturn and with bad luck. Disappointingly, the lead roll found in Eden Street contained no such curse. But it can still be viewed as a bad luck charm, thrown to the gods long ago by someone thirsting for revenge.

THE KINGSTON ISLAND

The departure of Rome's occupying forces from Britain in AD 410 left the country so vulnerable that local chiefs hired Anglo-Saxon mercenaries to fend off raiders from Ireland, Scotland and the North Sea coasts. Money had fallen out of use, so the newcomers were given land instead. Here they settled, multiplied, and eventually took control. This Saxon period produced the earliest known written reference to Kingston. It is a document of 838 which records an important council meeting held by King Egbert of Wessex in "that famous place which is called Kingston in the region of Surrey." Ironically, the era that saw the dawn of Kingston's recorded history and made it famous to this day as a residence and coronation place of Saxon kings, has yielded less archaeological evidence than any other period.

Why did the Saxons choose Kingston? Clues were

3. Preparing a medieval undercroft for lifting in December 1986.

4. An engineering feat that made international headlines – lifting a medieval undercroft in Kingston in December 1986.

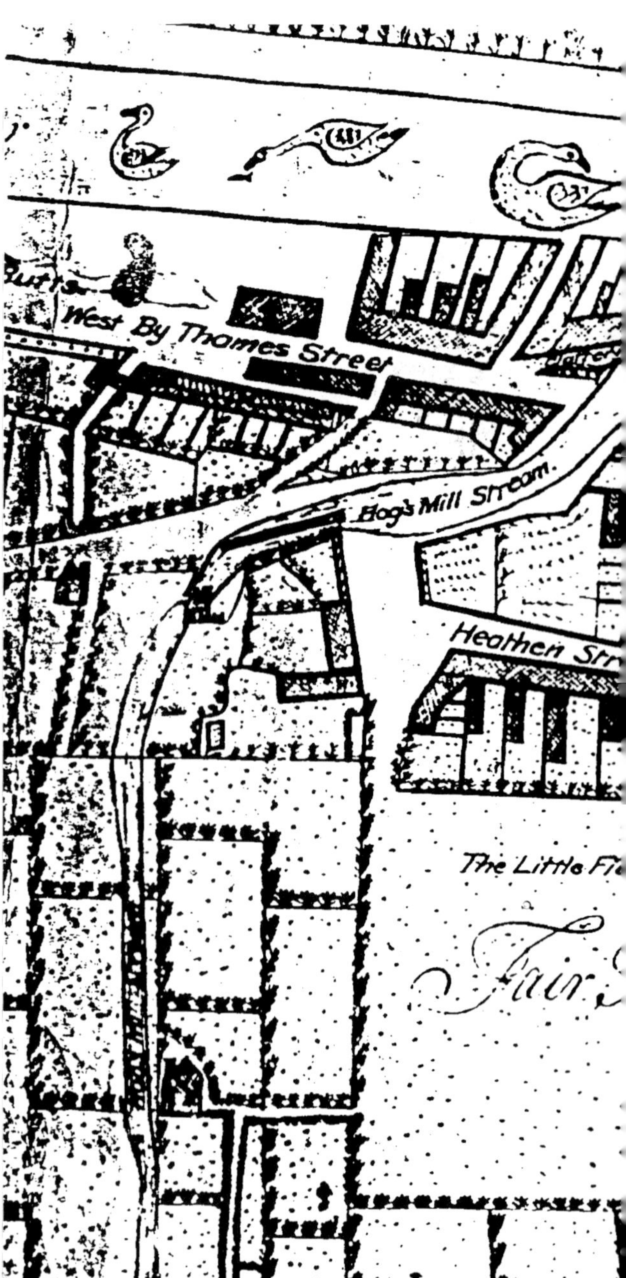

5. A seventeenth-century plan of Kingston. Names were added later, save for London Road and Fairfield.

unearthed in 1977, during archaeological excavations on the site of what is now the Eden Walk shopping precinct. There was evidence of people living here during the New Stone Age and the Bronze Age. But the most interesting discovery, leading to a major re-think of Kingston's past, was that a branch of the Thames flowed through Eden Walk 5,000 years ago, curving west to rejoin the main river near today's Down Hall Road. Thus, central Kingston was once a series of gravel islands, bounded by the Hogsmill, the Thames and the old Thames channel. This protective girdle of water and marsh made it a secure place for coronations and other key events attended by people of major importance. The core of modern Kingston – All Saints Church, the Market Place, Church Street – still stands on the former island where the town first took shape. And though the 'branch line' of the river slowly silted up over the centuries, it left a legacy of marshland that lasted until comparatively recent times, and dictated the siting of roads and buildings. A prime example is Eden Street, which got its curious bend because it was routed to skirt round the old watercourse and wetland.

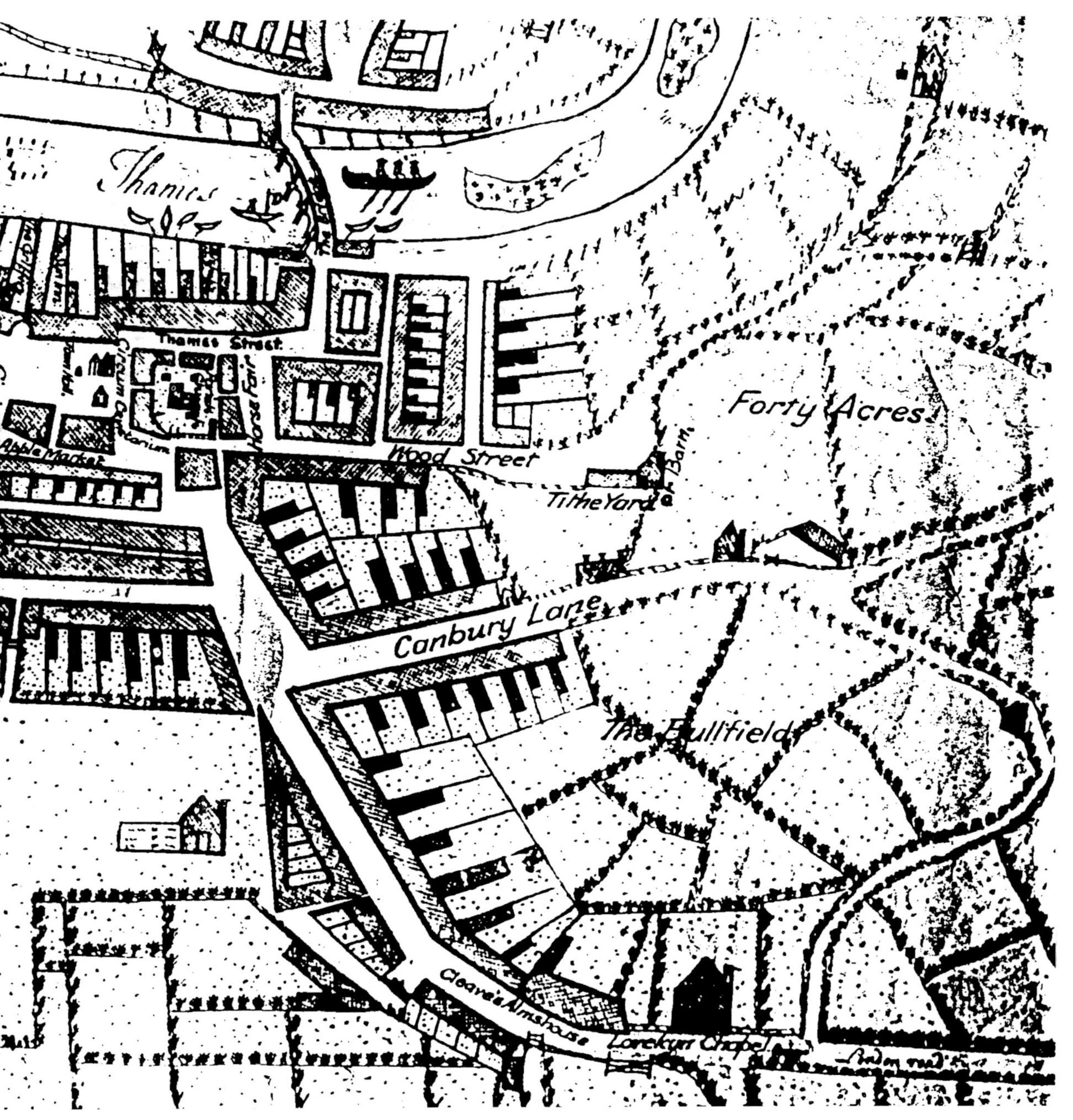
Thames
Thames Street
Horse Fair
Apple Market
Wood Street
Forty Acres
Barn
Tithe Yard
Canbury Lane
The Bullfield
Cleave's Almshouse
Lovekyn Chapel

Royal Kingston

There are only four Royal boroughs in England and Wales, and Kingston is the oldest. It was first described as a "royal town" by King Athelstan in a charter of 933, but was probably a royal seat at least a century before that. Kingston's main claim to royal status is the centuries-old tradition that seven Saxon kings were crowned here: Edward the Elder in 900; Athelstan in 925; Edmund in 940; Edred in 946; Edwy in 955; Edward the Martyr in 975 and Ethelred the Unready in 979. There is firm evidence for Athelstan and Ethelred, but the claims for the other five are less convincing. Some historians have also doubted if Kingston's Coronation Stone really is the sacred slab on which the elected monarchs were presented to their people. Nevertheless, it has been Kingston's most famous landmark since it was rescued from obscurity in 1850, set with coins from the reign of each of the kings supposed to have sat on it, and ringed with railings shaped like Saxon spears.

But the Stone did not, as commonly believed, inspire Kingston's name. That derives not from King's Stone, but King's Tun, meaning a royal estate. In a charter of 946, King Edred referred to "the Royal town which is called Kingston, where coronations are accustomed to be held"; in the Domesday Book of 1086, Kingston

6. In 1481 Edward IV granted Kingston official borough status, with the right to use a Corporation seal (depicted above).

7. Seven kings are reputed to have been crowned on Kingston's Coronation Stone, seen here by Clattern House at the turn of this century.

8. Kingston's earliest surviving charter – and the oldest document in the Borough Archives – is the one granted by King John in 1208.

9. Edward VII at Warren House, Kingston Hill, as a guest of General Sir Arthur Paget. He is pictured here in the loggia in May 1909. On his right is Lady Paget and R.B. Haldane MP, and on his left Mrs Spotswood and Lady Johnstone. Standing behind, from left to right, are his mistress, Mrs George Keppel; John Burns MP; Lady Hardinge; the Marquis de Soveral; Mrs Townsend; Ralph Paget; Henry Chaplin MP; Captain J.E. Paget; Col. Holford; General Sir Arthur Paget and Sir Charles Hardinge.

10. The Loyal Address sent by Kingston to Elizabeth II on the death of her father, George VI, in 1952.

TO

THE QUEEN'S MOST EXCELLENT MAJESTY.

THE LOYAL ADDRESS OF THE MAYOR, ALDERMEN AND BURGESSES OF THE ROYAL BOROUGH OF KINGSTON-UPON-THAMES.

MAY IT PLEASE YOUR MAJESTY.

We, Your Majesty's loyal and devoted Subjects, the Mayor, Aldermen and Burgesses of the Royal Borough of Kingston-upon-Thames in Council assembled, beg to tender our sorrow and heartfelt sympathy upon the lamented death of Your Illustrious Father, HIS MAJESTY KING GEORGE VI of gracious and happy memory.

Our beloved King, whom we do now so deeply mourn, was loved by us all for his wonderful devotion to the welfare of his subjects.

We beg respectfully to assure Your Majesty that the devoted loyalty with which we and all the Inhabitants of this Royal Borough have regarded our King now passed away, is tendered in unabated earnestness to Your Majesty.

And we pray that Your Majesty may long be spared to reign over us and to enjoy the blessings of Divine Providence in the fulfilment of the arduous functions devolving upon Your Majesty as the Constitutional Sovereign of the People of this Realm.

is described as a Royal manor, with a church, three salmon fisheries and five mills; and in 1481 Edward IV gave the town "a Common Seal to serve for things and business". It bore Kingston's ancient arms – a shield with three salmon – superimposed with the letter R to denote a Royal borough. These facts were quoted by the Mayor of Kingston, Alderman William Finny, when he petitioned George V in 1927 to confirm Kingston's status as a Royal borough. His Majesty granted the request.

In 1965, the boroughs of Kingston, New Malden and Surbiton were merged to form the new London Borough of Kingston upon Thames. The new body was granted the right to be called Royal in a charter issued by Elizabeth II in April that year.

11. Kingston Market Place is usually pictured looking north. This drawing of 1820 is a rare view south. On the left is the Tudor Guildhall, replaced in 1840. Most of the buildings on the right side – long known as High Row – are inns.

The Market Place

Kingston's Market Place has long been the focal point of the town. Its earliest record is in the Curia Regis Rolls of 1242, but clearly it was in existence well before then. It offered a wide range of merchandise. A Charter of 1448, in which Edward VI granted Kingston the right to charge tolls on goods passing over the bridge for sale in the town, lists more than two dozen items, including wine, hogs, timber, butter, salmon, salt, arrows, coal, cloth and iron. Deeds and rentals in the fourteenth and fifteenth centuries also show such names as Salteres Lane, Souters Row, Wool and Leather Market, The Butchery and Cook Row, which indicate the diversity of trade in and around the Market Place.

Kingston was also, from 1256, permitted to hold an annual fair, for eight days in November.

Kingston Market was strengthened by several Royal Charters, notably that of Charles I in 1628. This granted "that no other market shall from henceforth in future be created anew, or in any manner appointed, or in any way held in any place whatsoever within the distance of seven miles from the aforesaid town of Kingston-on-Thames, either through us, or any one, or any of our heirs or successors."

Such an extensive trading monopoly made it comparatively easy for Kingston to maintain the description by historian John Leland in 1535: "Kingston is the beste market towne of all Southery". This valuable seven-mile privilege still officially applies to the new borough boundaries, as it was extended by Royal Charter in 1965.

Only in the twentieth century has the Market operated six days a week. Previously trading was confined to Wednesdays, Thursdays and Saturdays, and stalls were dismantled after use, leaving a convenient open space for festivities, public punishments, proclamations and announcements.

Kingston's weekly Cattle Market moved from Market Place to the Fairfield in 1925, but was abandoned after the Second World War, when most local farmland had been swallowed by housing. But a general market is still held on the site each Monday.

12. Kingston Market Place, sketched by Thomas Rowlandson in about 1800.

13. Kingston's weekly Cattle Market moved from Market Place to the Fairfield in 1925, but was abandoned after the Second World War, when most local farmland had been swallowed up by housing. A general market is still held on the site each Monday. This picture was taken in the 1930s.

14. Kingston Market in the 1890s. Horse omnibuses share the road with goods carts and elegant carriages like the one on the left. Its liveried driver has stopped outside Joseph Hide's emporium and department store, which adjoined the Sun Hotel, and was patronised by Royalty – hence the Royal arms displayed on the first floor frontage. The white marble statue of a woman and child marks the Shrubsole Memorial – a drinking fountain erected in memory of Henry Shrubsole, thrice Mayor of Kingston, who died suddenly while distributing tea to the aged poor in 1880.

15. This view, looking south over Market Place, was photographed in the 1930s. The Market Place was pedestrianised in 1984.

16. This picture of 1985 shows the last Monday Market to be held on the Fairfield, before work began on the new Bus Station and Cattle Market car park. The market subsequently returned on a reduced site, and is still a weekly event.

Kingston Bridge

The earliest documentary reference to a Thames bridge at Kingston is in 1193, and riverside excavations in the 1980s revealed twelfth-century bridge remains, with high quality masonry. It is not known if this was the first bridge here, but it was certainly an important one; for it was the first bridge over the Thames above London, and therefore of strategic and economic importance.

Despite its stone revetments, the bridge was a flimsy wooden structure, as may be seen in the illustration below, constantly in need of repair. It was also extremely narrow.

An Act of 1825 authorised the building of a new stone bridge fifty yards upstream. Designed by Edward Lapidge, it took three years to construct and many buildings were demolished to make the approach road. Until then all through traffic had come down London Road into Wood Street, before curving left into Bridge Street, over the rotting timbers of the bridge, and into the Bridge Street continuation on the Hampton Wick side.

The new bridge was opened by the Duchess of Clarence on 17 July, 1828, and the new approach road was named Clarence Street in her honour.

17. Excavations in the 1980s revealed the twelfth-century remains of Kingston Bridge.

18. The medieval bridge was a flimsy and narrow affair. Despite its stone revetments, the superstructure was made of wood, and was in need of frequent repair.

19. The new Kingston Bridge, opened in 1828. This photograph was taken from the Middlesex bank in about 1890.

20. The twelfth-century Clattern bridge spans the Hogsmill between Kingston Market Place and High Street. This picture was taken in 1934, shortly before the Hogsmill was culverted, and a concrete 'platform' built over the water to form a setting for the Coronation Stone and the new Guildhall.

Early Pleasures

Until the nineteenth century people had virtually no leisure except on Church festival days. They had Sundays off, but were fined if they failed to attend church. One of many examples in the Kingston Bailiff's minute book is an entry of 1706: "Thomas Smith paid 5s for tippleing on the 5th day of May being ye Lord's day in time of Divine service." And the Churchwardens' Accounts of 1625 record "Recd on Sabbath dayes for idle persons being absent from church, 3s 10d." Working on Sundays was also punished. Joseph Wyght, a Kingston barber, faced the magistrates in 1690 for "trimming of Henry Deale in time of divine service... being ye Lord's Day."

Leisure time was further diminished in the fifteenth and sixteenth centuries by the duty of able-bodied men to practise archery. An Act of 1477 obliged a man to be equipped with a bow of his own height and to practise shooting at the town butts after Divine Service on Sundays and Holy days. Kingston archives contain a document of 1565 in which the town leased out one acre of the 'Teynter Field' (in the Bittoms area) provided that the lessee shall "leave suffycyent waye for ye Archers to go yn and owt to a Rounde standying and being in and uppon the seid acre of land above letten at ye east ende thereof nereunto the highway there leadying from Surpeton to Hogges Myll to pastyme and shoote at ye saide Rounde at all tyme".

21. Kingston's medieval Kyngham Game as depicted on a fifteenth-century playing card.

It is hardly surprising that when Kingstonians did have a few hours' freedom they enjoyed themselves with such abandon that authority was forced to intervene.

Jousts and other armed sports were favourite pastimes in medieval Kingston, but they could become too boisterous. In 1273 and again in 1274, the Patent Rolls record that Edward I ordered the cancellation of tournaments in the town. The churchyard was a popular sportsground, until in 1393 the Bishop of Winchester issued a mandate stating that clergy and laiety used the churchyard for ball games, stone-throwing and other activities, and had caused such damage that "juggling, the performance of loose dances, ballad singing, the exhibiting of shows and spectacles and the celebration of other games in the churchyard" were to be banned on pain of excommunication.

The most colourful holiday customs of old Kingston were the games referred to in the Churchwardens' Accounts as The Kyngham, the Robin Hood, the Lord of Misrule, the May Game and the Hock Game. Money collections, or 'gaderynges' were made at these games and given to the churchwardens, who then settled all the expenses. Any surplus went towards the maintenance of the church. The Kyngham featured a King and Queen of May with their nine dancers and attendants. A stained glass window in Kingston Museum (a twentieth-century reproduction of a seventeenth-century design) depicts the Kyngham, and shows the characters and their costumes in detail.

Such games appear in the sixteenth century accounts, and cast interesting light on the cost of food, clothes and labour in Tudor times: 1506-7 - Paid for whet and malt and vele and motton and pygges and ges and coks for the Kyngham, 33s; 1508-9 - item paid for 11 women for their labor for 11 days, 5d; item paid to John Wonam for a lambe, 16d; item paid for 2 payre of shone for ye Moreys dauncers, 14d."

The Reformation ended this type of merrymaking, and for several generations pleasures were mainly of a do-it-yourself nature. As late as 1852, local historian William Biden remarked: "There are no places of public amusement or recreation in Kingston; and indeed the place is altogether more distinguished for what it has not than for what it has."

The Guildhall

For centuries, Kingston Guildhall stood in the centre of Market Place. The original Guildhall was probably built soon after Edward IV's 1481 Charter of Incorporation, which gave Kingston official borough status. This building, seen here in a watercolour of about 1800, was refurbished in 1706, and embellished with the gilded statue of Queen Anne, sculpted by Francis Bird for £47 8s 6d, which has gazed over the Market Place ever since.

From this building Kingston was governed by a Court of Assembly, consisting of two Bailiffs, a High Steward, a Recorder, Gownsmen, Peers and fifteen Headboroughs, or Constables. The Municipal Corporations Act of 1835 replaced the Court of Assembly structure with a Borough Council.

In 1838 the dilapidated Guildhall was demolished and rebuilt to a design by Charles Henman; the Queen Anne statue was transferred to the front of the new building, which opened in 1840.

The year 1902 was the bicentenary of Queen Anne's coronation. The seven-times mayor of Kingston, Ald. William Finny, marked the anniversary by paying from his own pocket for the statue to be repaired and re-gilded. It was then ceremoniously unveiled by the Japanese minister, Viscount Hayashi.

By 1891 the Council had outgrown its Guildhall and several departments were transferred to Clattern House, an eighteenth-century mansion to the south of the Market Place, adjoining the Assize Courts. Further municipal expansion resulted in the demolition of Clattern House and the adjoining buildings in 1933 to make way for the present Guildhall. This was opened on 3 July 1935 by Princess Alice, Countess of Athlone. The old Guildhall then became the Market House.

In 1993 the Market House closed for a £650,000 facelift. When it reopened in 1995 it had been restored to its original beauty inside and out. The handsome former Council Chamber can now be hired for functions, and there is a café and information desk on the ground floor.

The 1.3 ton lead statue of Queen Anne was removed to Wandsworth for months of restoration by Plowden & Smith. They found the Queen filthy and

22. *Kingston Guildhall and Market Place, by Thomas Rowlandson, 1800.*

23. *'Kingston Market House, c.1840', by C. Henman and T.J. Rawlins.*

24. *The Guildhall was decorated with dozens of coloured gas lamps for Queen Victoria's Diamond Jubilee in 1897.*

25. Unveiling the renovated statue of Queen Anne in 1902. The restoration was the gift of seven-times Mayor of Kingston, Ald. William Finny.

26. In 1994, the statue was removed for extensive repairs. Queen Anne was repainted in gold leaf.

half bald with a broken wrist, a gown full of holes, and a hollow body filled with cement. It cost £15,500 to make the statue perfect and re-gild it with gold leaf. The cost was met by Bentalls, English Heritage, the Leslie Trust and the Heritage of London Trust.

27. In 1891 some of the Borough's departments were moved out of the Guildhall to Clattern House, an eighteenth-century mansion on the south side of the Market Place. The Assize Courts, built in 1811, are on the left, and to the far left was the town jail, which later became a public bathhouse and then, from 1897, a public lavatory.

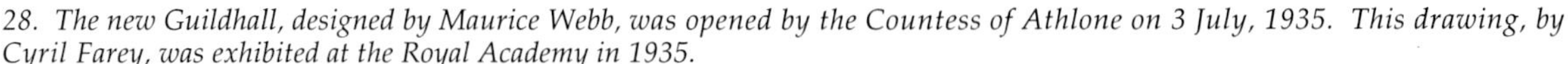

28. The new Guildhall, designed by Maurice Webb, was opened by the Countess of Athlone on 3 July, 1935. This drawing, by Cyril Farey, was exhibited at the Royal Academy in 1935.

Kingston at Prayer

ALL SAINTS

Christians have worshipped on the site of Kingston's All Saints Church for more than a thousand years. There has been a church here at least since 838, when King Egbert of Wessex held an important ecclesiastical council in "that renowned place which is called Cyninges-tun". A document of the time records that the first event of the meeting was a gift of land made "before the altar", indicating that a church existed there. This is doubtless the building referred to in the Coronation service of Ethelred II, crowned in Kingston in 979: "Two Bishops... shall lead the King to the church... when the King arrives at the church he shall prostrate himself before the altar."

The status of Kingston's Anglo-Saxon church is uncertain; but John Leland noted in the sixteenth century that local people had told him "that wher their toun chirche is now was sumtyme an abbey". Recent evidence suggests it was a minster. This church was dedicated to All Hallows, and probably destroyed by the Danes, who swept up the Thames in 1019, burning towns on both sides of the river. The only remnant of it is a part of an eighth-century stone cross.

The Danes plundered churches, then set fire to them, leaving only the bare walls. So when Gilbert the Norman built Kingston's cruciform church of All Saints in about 1130, he probably followed the usual Norman practice of incorporating the old nave walls into the new building, and built the tower on arches on the site of the previous Saxon chancel.

The Domesday Book of 1086 records that Kingston had a church. This was probably the Saxon chapel of St Mary, which adjoined the later All Hallows on its south side. It survived until 1730 when the sexton, Abram Hammerton, undermined its foundations while gravedigging. Part of the building collapsed, killing him and another man. His daughter, Esther, was also trapped, but was rescued alive to succeed her father as sexton. The remaining portion of the chapel was soon demolished by the parishioners, and the site left bare until 1825, when it was merged with the churchyard for burials and lost from sight. It was rediscovered in 1926 during excavations by Dr Finny, who was Mayor of Kingston seven times, High Steward of the borough, and a keen local historian. Fragments from the ancient walls were rebuilt, and the site marked out with metal plaques as a permanent memorial.

During the thirteenth and fourteenth centuries Merton Priory, which owned the living, retained

29. This seventeenth-century drawing by Daniel King is the only known picture of the wooden spire on Kingston Church, which was removed in 1703 after severe storm damage.

30. The interior of All Saints Church, looking west in the 1840s. During drastic alterations in the 1850s and 60s, the high boxed pews were removed, the plaster ceiling taken down to reveal the open timbered roof, and the organ gallery replaced by the fine west window. This depicts Christ in Majesty, with apostles modelled on local personalities of the time.

31. Esther Hammerton, who took over as sexton for Kingston, after her father's death when St Mary's Chapel collapsed on him.

32. All Saints Church in the early years of this century.

most of All Saints' income, leaving only a pittance to maintain the church and pay the vicar. Finally, in 1368 the Bishop of Winchester issued a mandate stating that the chancel at Kingston was in a serious state of disrepair, even though his predecessor had repeatedly ordered the priory to repair and re-roof it. Possibly it was due to this neglect that the Norman nave was rebuilt in the fourteenth century.

The tower at this time was surmounted by a lofty wooden spire, which was destroyed in "a great weathering of wind, hayle, snow, rayne and thunders with lightening" in 1445. It was rebuilt in 1505, but demolished (and never replaced) after the "great Winde and Hurricane" of 1703. The tower itself was strengthened and largely rebuilt in 1708, and again in 1973, but its thirteenth-century lower section survives.

After the Reformation and the dissolution of Merton Priory, the Kingston church fabric again deteriorated. To make matters worse, Edward VI despatched commissioners to churches throughout the land to seize every item of value "to the King's use". Two contingents of Royal commissioners stripped All Saints of vestments, plate and other treasures, and when a third arrived he found only two chalices had been spared, but "there remained to the kinges use fyve great belles in the steple, a suns (sanctus) bell, and a chyme for the belles." There were more indignities during the Civil Wars, when Roundhead troops used the church as a stable, smashed the pews and destroyed monuments and tablets.

In 1699, a vestry meeting reported that the building was almost ruinous, and a rate of 6d in the pound was levied in the parish to pay for repairs. The church has been altered several times since then, notably in the nineteenth century. In 1997 it was announced that the building was urgently in need of repairs and modernisation costing more than £2 million. This work included basic sanitary facilities. The churchwardens in 1635 had paid 3s for a pewter chamber pot for use in church. In 1997 the building still had no lavatory or running water! All Saints' long reign as the only parish church in Kingston ended in 1842 with the opening of St Peter's, Norbiton. As the local population grew – largely through the advent of railways – other churches followed. Today there are fourteen churches in the Kingston deanery.

33. Kingston Baptist Church in the 1860s. Adjoining it is the building that opened in 1825 as the town watch house, and later became Kingston Mortuary.

34. The building shown above was superseded by a new Baptist church in 1864. The old mortuary, which still adjoins it, was converted into a shop in the 1930s by adding an upper floor and 'Tudorbethan' embellishments. It adjoins the Garden of Remembrance.

NONCONFORMISTS

Nonconformists have a long history in Kingston. This is largely due to Dr Edmund Staunton, who became vicar of Kingston in 1631 and retained the position for some twenty years – despite being suspended from the ministry for a time in 1634 because of his Puritan views. He sided with Presbyterians during the Civil Wars, and eventually became president of Corpus Christi College, Oxford. However, after the Restoration he was expelled from the church for his nonconformity.

Dr Staunton left three lasting memorials in Kingston. One is the brass plaque in All Saints Church commemorating his ten children, who all died in infancy. The others are Kingston's Congregational and Baptist churches, both of which have their origins in the Presbyterian doctrines he instilled into his young clerical assistant, Richard Mayo. In 1659 Mayo succeeded his master as Vicar of Kingston, but in 1662 he was expelled from the living and began preaching to a group of parish church rebels who held secret religious meetings in each other's houses. By 1669 the Episcopal Returns noted that the group had grown to a hundred members.

In 1672 the Act of Indulgence enabled nonconformists to meet openly. A house owned by John Pigot in Kingston was licensed as a Presbyterian meeting house, with Mayo as its minister. He left in 1687, but the group continued to flourish, and by about 1690 had its own meeting house in Brick Lane (later renamed Union Street). The work of Staunton and Mayo received fresh impetus in 1698, when Richard Mayo's son, Daniel, took over the Kingston Presbyterian ministry. He served there until his death in 1733; but the congregation dwindled under his successor, George Whightwick. There were disagreements, and in 1775 the members split, one group eventually founding a Baptist church in Brick Lane, and the other a Congregational church in Eden Street.

THE QUAKERS

The oldest nonconformist group in Kingston are the Quakers. George Fox, founder of the movement, came here many times, and by the 1650s a Kingston miller named John Fielder was risking savage punishment by holding Quaker meetings at his house, the Hand in Hand. This building, described as an inn and a granary, stood on what is now the Garden of Remembrance in Church Street. Freedom of worship was forbidden for much of the seventeenth century, and people were obliged by law to worship at the parish church, or be fined for non-attendance. Then Conventicle Acts were passed in 1664 and 1670 making it illegal to hold religious meetings anywhere but in the parish church.

This meant that Kingston's two nonconformist groups, the Quakers and Presbyterians, had to meet

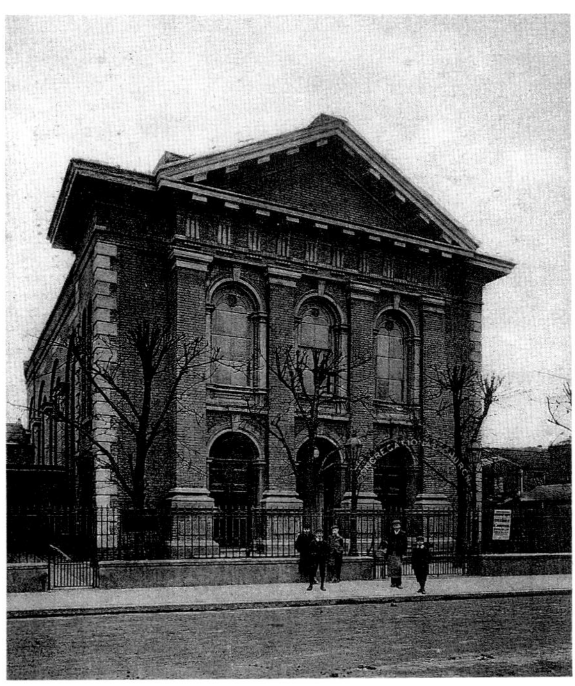

35. Kingston Congregational Church (now Kingston United Reformed Church) in 1905.

secretly and members were frequently jailed and fined. Nevertheless, the Quakers flourished and in the 1670s built a meeting house on the corner of Eden Street and Union Street. Here they met for more than a century before moving to their present premises in 1781. Something of their suffering is revealed in their surviving documents. For example this, written in 1670: ''And when Friends have been kept out of their [Kingston] meeting room, Captain Edward Brett`s Soldiers have come and brought Sticks and struck Friends in a cruel manner and puncht them with their carbines on the Brest and Backs. Christopher White they puncht on the Brest so that the bloud burst out of his Nose; and severall others they puncht and beat so that they were sore a great while after... and it has been the Soldiers practice (Meeting after Meeting as Constantely as Friends mett) to come and beat and punch Friends in a Cruel and Barbarous manner...''

Troops and Corporation officers also raided Quaker homes and made "havock and spoil" of their goods. On one occasion there was a raid on the home of Thomas Tanner. While Mrs Tanner and her seven small children watched in terror, Corporation officers stripped the home "and left them so bare that they were faine to lie upon Matts." Other Quakers were even more humiliated. The town's bailiffs broke up one meeting themselves, and threw two of the Friends in jail "and put four Friends in ye Cage where use to put Beggars, when they take them up in order to whipp them."

After the Friends moved to their present site in Eden Street, their empty building was taken over by the Congregationalists, who named it the "meeting house in the Back Lane" and when the lease expired, they put up their own premises next door. These in turn were replaced in 1855 by the church that stands today, though altered and much restored in the 1970s. It became the United Reformed Church following the merger between Presbyterians and Congregationalists in 1972.

THE SALVATIONISTS

It was winter 1886 when the Salvation Army first invaded Kingston. By then the Army, formed in 1865, had more than 900 corps and were still expanding. The officers sent to win over Kingston were two young sisters, Captain Charlotte Jackson and Lieutenant Agnes Jackson, who began their campaign one Sunday morning. Their only troops were a cadet, plus six soldiers from adjacent areas. The Lyceum, a meeting hall in Union Street, had been taken on a year's lease by the Army as their Kingston barracks. Knee-drill (prayers) was held here at 7am before the Jackson sisters marched out to the nearby Market Place for two hours of open-air 'firing' (preaching). This outraged people on their way to church, and was an irresistible challenge to the roughs of the town, who had already publicly announced that they would inflict "a defeat with great slaughter" on the two "hallelujah lasses" and their supporters. "The conduct of the crowd was most disgraceful, for besides molesting members of the Army, those who were nearest to them assailed them with the most horrible blasphemy", reported the *Surrey Comet*. The Army`s newspaper, *War Cry*, described events at The Lyceum under the heading 'Stormy Times': "The morning meeting was a treat. The hall was packed to excess and amid cries, tumult and disorder, we managed an occasional hearing. The afternoon meeting was broken up. Complete disorder ensured; smoking, stump speeches and a series of questions were asked and answered from the enemy's ranks. Salvationists were completely at the mercy of the populace, and but for the kindly intervention of the police, threats most serious could and doubtless would have been put in force. The evening meeting was somewhat of a different character. But outside, although an inspector and a body of police were present, from one to two thousand filled the streets and a steady fire of rotten eggs and other missiles, glass smashed, groans and yells swelled the songs inside... Keep believing. Victory, happiness and Heaven shall greet and cheer thousands in Kingston-on-Thames, Lord hasten the day... Two brothers met with a warm reception in the shape of a bag of flour each as a first greeting.

36. Agnes and Charlotte Jackson, who led the Salvation Army's 'invasion' into Kingston.

37. Kingston's Salvation Army Songsters outside the newly-built Kingston Guildhall in the 1930s.

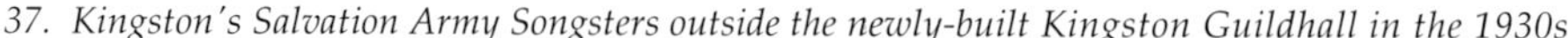

38. St Raphael's Church.

We all came back to the barracks covered with flour. Inside we had a good meeting, and God showed Himself the Victor by releasing three from slavery... Sunday was another glorious day. Afternoon, good meeting, one soul saved; evening, real Salvation meeting, much conviction. Seven came to the world's redeemer."

Despite all, the Army expanded steadily in Kingston, quitting the Lyceum for permanent premises in Elm Road, and hiring the Cinem Palace picture theatre in Richmond Road for Sunday services. Nevertheless, their early bands were a great trial to the town as the unskilled musicians blew hunting horns, strummed banjos, tooted cornets and beat drums like men possessed. But by 1904 the Kingston band was described as the Army's best, and its music gave public pleasure for years. The opening of the large Salvation Army Citadel in Fairfield Road in 1930 heralded community work on a much larger scale, working in co-operation with other churches and the local authority. Today the Kingston Corps is struggling to meet ever-increasing demands on its services at a time when social pressures and urban redevelopment schemes have forced large sections of the soldiery out of the area.

A CATHOLIC'S DILEMMA

More than three centuries after the Reformation, Kingston still had no Roman Catholic church. That gap was filled in an unusual way when Alexander Raphael, the first Roman Catholic to become Sheriff of London after the Catholic Emancipation Act, fell gravely ill at Surbiton Hall, his stately mansion in Kingston.

He recovered, against all the odds, and his medical adviser, Dr Sudlow Roots, warned that his bill would be heavy because the illness had been so long. Mr Raphael retorted that his recovery was no thanks to the doctor, but to the fact that he had vowed to the Virgin Mary that if she would intercede for his recovery, he would build a church at the then great cost of £7,000. The result was the beautiful little St Raphael's Church, completed on his riverside estate in 1848. But Mr Raphael never worshipped there. He continued to attend Mass at Richmond because he had a dream which foretold his death soon after the consecration of his own church. He therefore deferred the ceremony as long as possible. Several appointments were made with Bishop Nicholas Wiseman, head of what was then known as the London District, and each time they were cancelled. This continued until 1850 when, once again, arrangements were made for the consecration. This time Mr Raphael, by some oversight, did not revoke them. Bishop Wiseman arrived on the appointed day with his chaplain, Monsignor Francis Searle. He found the church locked, and Mr Raphael away. However, the butler produced the key, and the Bishop went ahead with the ceremony, accompanied only by Monsignor Searle. Raphael was aghast when he found what had happened. He sacked the butler but died soon after, just as his dream had foretold. Now his remains lie in a brass-studded coffin beneath the High Altar of the church he never used.

The year of Raphael's death was also the year the Pope decreed that Bishop Wiseman should become the first Archbishop of Westminster. Mr Gower, a curate at All Saints, inflamed Kingston with a sermon condemning the Pope's "usurpation of authority in this realm". Enraged parishioners then made an effigy of the new Cardinal and paraded it round the streets of Kingston before burning it on the Fairfield.

Charitable Endeavours

TACKLING ABUSES

Few small towns had such a multitude of charitable endowments as Kingston, and few could have abused them so thoroughly. There were more than twenty, and in earlier years they had done sterling work in providing education and grants to the poor. But by the 1860s many were blatantly mismanaged. Every type of confidence trickster, scrounger and down-and-out came to Kingston for the enormous number of handouts. To get residential qualification they were prepared to take any type of hovel, and unscrupulous charity trustees made a fortune renting out shacks of indescribable filth and squalor. Alderman Frederick Gould, a prominent townsman who campaigned for the charities to be put in order, recalled the "regular drunken orgy" that accompanied the handouts. "The gifts consisted of tickets entitling the holders to jackets, trousers, boots, flannels, bedding and various other things. There was a cursing, fighting, disorderly mob, and the scenes were shocking to witness... as soon as the applicants got the tickets, a very large proportion of them sold the tickets, went to the nearest public house and spent the money in drink."

Gould led such a vigorous campaign against these abuses that eventually the income from eight bequests was pooled for education. The result was the rebuilding of the then dying Kingston Grammar School – whose own endowments had been plundered by unscrupulous councillors years before – and the founding of the Tiffin Schools. Both are now among the best schools of their kind in Britain.

CLEAVE'S ALMSHOUSES

Most of Kingston's remaining charities were merged in 1874; but one retains a separate identity as Cleave's Almshouses. William Cleave, in his will of 1665, left money "for the erecting and building of a convenient house" for "six poor men and six poor women of honest life and reputation". His wishes were carried out to the letter, and Cleave's Almshouses, built in 1669, extended in 1889, and substantially refurbished and modernised in 1994, survive to this day in London Road. They are administered by Kingston United Charities, set up in 1931. The same organisation is also responsible for nine more ancient charities, now merged to provide a small annual income.

39. Cleave's Almshouses.

40. The Cambridge Asylum for Soldiers' Widows in 1852. The site is now occupied by local authority housing.

THE ROYAL CAMBRIDGE

A particularly worthwhile memorial was Kingston's Royal Cambridge Asylum. It was built in memory of the lst Duke of Cambridge, who owned thousands of acres in the area, and had also been Commander-in-Chief of the British Army. Thus it was decided that the asylum should be specifically for soldiers' widows, who received no statutory benefits at that time, and often became destitute. The 2nd Duke of Cambridge gave a landscaped site in Norbiton Park, and nearly £4,000 was raised by public subscription. In June 1852 the Prince Consort laid the foundation stone of what was later described by the Press as "a noble monument of English charity". It was designed in Elizabethan style by architect Thomas Allom to house 160 residents. The Royal family, notably Queen Mary, kept a keen interest in the project until it was badly damaged in World War II. The residents were moved elsewhere, and after the war the building was demolished to make way for council flats. Only its entrance lodge remains.

THE METROPOLITAN AND THE PRINCESS LOUISE

Kingston had a gala day in 1875 when the Prince and Princess of Wales (later Edward VII and Queen Alexandra) came to open the Metropolitan Convalescent Institution home on Kingston Hill. This offered free accommodation for up to 150 poor children recovering from serious illness, and promised "a plentiful, wholesome diet, fresh air and country scenes" at a time when Kingston Hill could indeed claim to be rural. Though decried by later generations, the building was a model of its kind at that time. Designed in neo-medieval style by the eminent architect, Saxon Snell, it cost the then vast sum of £10,000 to build, plus £1,500 for the site, and a further large sum for furnishings and the most modern of fittings, such as Jennings' patent lavatory basins, and Benham's patent cooking apparatus. In 1892 this distinctive building, with a 90-foot water tower in the centre, was bought by the National Society for the Protection of Young Girls, and opened by Princess Louise as a home "to save young girls between the ages of 11 and 15, from any part of the kingdon, whether orphans or otherwise, who are from any circumstances exposed to temptation, or in danger of being abandoned... to educate, train, feed, clothe and prepare them for future usefulness as domestic servants, to procure situations for them, provide them with an outfit, and generally watch over, advise and counsel them... to reward them for continued good conduct in service, and in every possible way to become their guardians."

There are still old residents who remember the girls

41. Men of the Duke of Cambridge's Hussars formed a guard of honour for the Duke of Cambridge when he came to open the Victoria Hospital in 1898 (see p77). Watching from behind the hedge are white-capped inmates of Kingston Workhouse.

from the Princess Louise home, as it was called. They wore starched white aprons, and delivered laundry to local houses in handcarts. The home, which existed on donations and the proceeds from laundry work, was forced to close in 1933 through lack of funds.

DR BARNARDO'S

The Princess Louise home was then bought by Lady Dalziel of Wooler and presented to the Dr Barnardo organisation as a home for 150 boys. Author Leslie Thomas was sent there in 1943 as a 12-year-old orphan and, in his book *This Time Next Week*, remembers the iron rule of the superintendent, Ernest Gardiner. He also remembers "long, smelly, echoing corridors, windows in the iron-bedded dormitories still covered with plywood and cardboard after being blown out by the blitz... each morning we breakfasted on two slices of bread and dripping and a mug of unsweetened cocoa. At teatime two further rounds, spread with margarine, were put before us with a mug of tea. A dozen rather grizzled spinsters were in charge of the dormitories, each with a cell of a room on the landing outside. They were well-meaning enough (though the sickroom matron packed a deft left hook) but they probably needed a home as much as we did. Yet, for all of that, to us it was HOME. It was all we had. When boys left, and went to work, they were frequently back, strutting in their newly-issued suits, the following weekend."

The home closed in 1968. Soon afterwards it was demolished, and replaced by the townhouses of Blenheim Gardens. Dr Barnardo himself had died nearby in Surbiton 63 years previously, having spent his final weeks in an agonising time race across Europe so that he could die at St Leonard's Lodge, his house near the river in Portsmouth Road. The house, where his wife declared they spent their happiest years, has been replaced by Ravensview Court, a block of flats with nothing external to commemorate the remarkable man who lived there. This would pique Dr Barnardo, a man who always craved, but in his lifetime never achieved, official recognition of his achievements. By the time he died in 1905 he had rescued nearly 60,000 children, sacrificing his health to the work he began in 1867.

42. *The Matron (Miss Skinner) and staff of the Princess Louise Home, Kingston Hill in 1913.*

43. *Dr Thomas Barnardo with his sons, Stuart and Herbert.*

44. *Originally the Metropolitan Institution, then the Princess Louise Home, this building was acquired for Dr Barnardo's Homes in 1933.*

Law and Order

THE LOCAL BEAT

Crime was a problem in medieval Kingston. For example, in 1399 criminals caused such havoc in the town that the residents petitioned King Edward III, who ordered an investigation "as the town was lately burned by certain malefactors and all the goods and chattels there were plundered and destroyed". Seven years later, the King was condemning "divers homicides, robberies and other felonies perpetrated daily by men called roberdsmen, wasturs and draghlaches", adding that "the constables are negligent... and the said men by day and night run about perpetrating the evils aforesaid." A crime squad was formed, headed by Thomas de Purle, John de Codeston and John Scot of Kingston, and the Sheriff and other county officials were ordered to help arrest and keep in custody "all those of whom there is suspicion of ill".

But crime continued to mount, largely because there were no paid police. Instead, every householder had to take his turn at 'watching in the night'. Each watch had a constable, eight men and the town's bellman and beadle. The bellman kept the rota, warning each man when it was his turn to serve and, with the beadle, kept a fire and candle burning in the watch-house and arranged substitutes for the majority of householders who were only too glad to pay 6d for someone else – usually a down-and-out – to take their place.

By the eighteenth century, to quote William Biden, "every vice and every species of immorality was practised more or less openly", and in 1773 Parliament passed the Act for the Lighting and Watching of Kingston. This authorised the Corporation to appoint up to fourteen paid watchmen, who could be armed at night. But the Corporation took little advantage of the Act. The number of watchmen, known as 'old Charlies', was usually well below strength and they were always a motley crew. In 1897 Philip Jones recalled them seventy years earlier: "They gathered at 10pm when the curfew bell was rung, and they would sing out "past ten o`clock and a moonlight night" and then hurry off to find the nearest drinking booth. There used to be watchboxes at various corners, and some rare fun we used to have with the old Charlies... as they used to frequently sleep while on duty, it was a standing joke for the young sparks to turn over the watchbox with the Charlie inside it." One Charlie had a wooden leg. Another was so old and small that as he shuffled along his lantern dragged the ground.

It was the custom in Kingston for Fifteens (councillors) automatically to become Headboroughs (constables) when they were elected to the Corporation.

45. This building was constructed in 1825 as a watch-house where Kingston's 'Charlies' – early policemen – could collect their bludgeons and lanterns each night. It was converted into a mortuary and then a shop in 1939 by Mr Gausten, a tailor. In 1950 he added an upper floor and mock Tudor timbering. The shop is now a patisserie. This picture was taken in the 1970s.

As they were untrained, unpaid, and forced to serve against their will, their work was so inefficient that in 1823 they were charged at Kingston Quarter Sessions with gross neglect of their duties. A Parliamentary Commission of 1834 was appalled to find that the Headboroughs had become nominal figures, and that three paid constables and three watchmen were the entire police force of Kingston town: "These six are the only effective town officers. There is no system of police", it stated. In 1835, the Borough Police Act compelled Kingston to set up a Watch Committee and reorganise its watching system on the lines of the Metropolitan Police. The new committee decided to add five paid constables "making the whole number with those at present on the watch nine constables". Day constables were to be paid a weekly 18s, night watchmen 14s, and they were to be "cloathed in an uniform manner, with blue coats, waistcoats, trousers, glazed hats, oil skin capes and great coats... the night constables to carry for their protection, and those of the inhabitants, a cutlass, rattle, dark lanthorn, and a staff... they should go their rounds silently and without calling the hour." Their headquarters continued to be under the old town hall, and the watch-house built in Union Street

46. Kingston police force, 1888.

in 1825 continued as the chief rallying point for the night watch.

With the growing threat that the Metropolican Police would take over the policing of Kingston, the Council worked feverishly to provide a new, purpose-built police station near Clattern Bridge. But in 1839 an Act of Parliament brought Kingston within the Metropolitan Police district. An enraged Corporation found that the so-called 'new police' did not want its new police station, nor its able head constable, Richard Cook. The station was let at a peppercorn rent to the Association for Bettering the Condition of the Poor, and Cook, described as "a smart man who was the dread of thieves and poachers" was sacked. The watch-house in Union Street became the town mortuary. (Today, much altered, it is a cake shop.)

A new police station was built in London Road in 1864. It remained Kingston's police HQ until 1968, when new premises were built alongside the Guildhall.

EXTREME PUNISHMENTS

When criminals *were* brought to book in Kingston, their punishments could be fierce. In earlier centuries, stocks, pillory and a whipping post were kept in the Market Place. Public burnings were also carried out there, while hanging usually took place on a stretch of open land at the top of Kingston Hill. The parish register for 8 September, 1572, records: "This day in this towne....was hangid six persons and seventeen taken for roges and vagabonds and whippid abowte the market place and brent in the ears".

The seventeenth-century Chamberlains' Accounts include: 1613, a whip for Rogues; 1615, tow planks to make a pair of Stocks; 1634, a vizard and cap for the whipper; 1636, stuffe and worke done at the Courthall pillory; 1681, thirty-three foot of timber "to make the gallows" and "to three men for bringing one hundred of Bavins and fifty fagotts to burne ye woman, 4s."

Records of Assizes held in Kingston during the eighteenth and nineteenth centuries are full of hangings and transportations to the Colonies. Examples include Mary Langsden, hanged in 1753 for stealing a purse; Charles Manmore sentenced to death in 1833 for stealing a horse; and Samuel Rose, transported for seven years for taking a ring.

Typical examples from Kingston Bailiffs' Minute books for the eighteenth century include: 1705, John Turner and John Mitchell, who stole two neckcloths, from a hedge, both "listed into her majesties service"; 1707, Dorothy Terrill set in ye stocks for swearing; 1710, Ann Saunders "Drunk a Sunday by her owne Confession Ordered to ye stocks for two houres if she can`t pay 5s". But the most dramatic sentence was reported in the *European Magazine* of 1795: "Very near 30 years ago a remarkable execution happened at Kingston in Surrey. One Gregory was hanged for horse stealing, and at the same time no less than 11 of his own sons were hung by his side on the same gallows for repeated crimes of the same nature; and what is yet more singular, one Colman, with his five sons, were hung on the same gallows at the same moment, in all 18 in number."

There was a special punishment for bad-tempered women in Kingston. This was the ducking stool, a chair which hung from an axle attached to the end of two long poles. The whole contraption was mounted on three wheels so the victim could be tied to the seat, and wheeled publicly through the town to Kingston Bridge.

An early account of a ducking appears in the parish registers: "1572 August. On Tewsday being the xix of this monthe of August... Downing... wyfe to... Downing gravemaker of this parysshe she was sett on a new cukking stolle made of a grett hythe and so browght a bowte the markett place to Temes brydge and ther had 111 duckings over hed and eres becowse she was a common scolde and fyghter``

In 1738 the *Universal Spectator* carried a report of an Kingston alewife sentenced at the Quarter Sessions to a ducking. It was duly carried out "and to prove the justice of the court's sentence upon her, on her return from the waterside she fell upon one of her acquaintances, without provocation, with tongue, tooth and nail and, had not the officers interposed, would have deserved a second punishment even before she was dry from the first."

Use of the ducking stool had ceased by the nineteenth century, but for some years scolds were publicly humiliated by having the old stool propped up outside their homes.

47. Kingston's Debtors' Prison at the Hand and Mace; it was pulled down in 1831.

KINGSTON PRISONS

Kingston had two prisons, both grim. One was the debtors' gaol, known as the Stockhouse, run by licensed victuallers who were allowed to operate an alehouse there in lieu of salary. The punishment meted to those in debt is described in a letter published in the *Gentleman's Magazine* in 1804, written by James Neild, who had visited the gaol: "I found one Richard Holt confined for a debt of £6 6s, costs £3 3s 9d. This poor man told me he had brought up a wife and ten children without parochial assistance; but having been in confinement eleven weeks, his wife and three youngest children were in the workhouse... there is no allowance whatever, not even water accessible to the prisoner; there is a narrow slip, of fourteen feet long by three feet wide, with an iron-grated window towards the street. In this the prisoner stands to beg; and, but for the casual interference of humane individuals, can no longer exist than human nature can do without food. The late keeper informed me he had frequently made application to the bailiffs of the borough for a daily allowance, but was always told there was none for them. The gaoler, W. Walter, is a sheriff's officer. He has no salary, but keeps a tap in lieu. Thus is a licensed alehouse become a necessary part of the prison establishment by being made a means of its finance. Fees 3s 4d. No chaplain, or any religious attentions. Surgeon, Mr Taylor, salary none; makes a bill. For poor debtors there is one room 18 feet by 14 feet and 6 feet 6 inches high and adjoining to the slip above mentioned. As the Corporation allows neither bed nor bedding, the keeper has humanely furnished the poor inoffensive man with a bedstead, mattress, blanket and rug; in return for which the prisoner did any little jobs which the nature of his confinement would allow. Above stairs are four rooms, none well furnished, for those who can pay 7s 6d per week. Another room, furnished in an inferior manner, at 2s 6d a week. The two other rooms have no bedsteads or beds in them, but are appropriated to felons at the assize. And the keeper informed me that 24 felons have been crowded (like sheep in a pen) for two or three days into a room 19 feet by 9. They are fastened down to staples fixed in the floor by a ponderous iron chain run through the main link of their fetters. One blanket is allowed to each prisoner. Rooms dirty, and not whitewashed.

The prison and alehouse, built by the Corporation in about 1505, were pulled down in 1831 when the street was widened to make an approach to the new Kingston Bridge. A new debtors' prison was built in what is now Bath Passage. This was later converted to a bath house.

Kingston also had Surrey's County Gaol, or House of Correction, opened in 1761 off what is now Lady Booth Road. James Neild's impressions of it also appeared in the *Gentleman's Magazine* in 1804. He reported that prisoners had "scanty" rations, allowed one pound of bread each per day with only water to drink. "There is a house for the keeper (William Matthews, salary £45) and separate wards for men and women, with separate courts, work-sheds and pumps. Each ward has two lower rooms three steps above the ground, and two rooms above. The men's rooms are 16 feet by 14, and 9 feet high; the women's about 15 feet square; every room planked round; a chimney in each, and two windows with shutters and iron bars; no glass except in two, which are appropriated to the sick. The men's court is 59 feet by 50; the women's 46 by 36. There is also a room quite separate for faulty apprentices, about 8 feet by 11, and 8 feet high; it has a fireplace. There is a bathing tub in each court. The county allows nothing but straw to lie upon. Prisoners on June 19, 1802 were 18 men, 4 women... 11 were committed to hard labour, and for which there is in each court a convenient work-shed; yet not one of them was employed, or any attention paid to the means of industry. No firing allowed in winter." Mr Neild added that the prison was "very clean". Inside the gate was painted "no admittance in church time. No garnish to be taken. If any prisoner strike another, complain to the keeper. If any prisoner shall be guilty of profane cursing or swearing, or any indecent behaviour, complain to the keeper."

The Gaol Returns of 1841 praised the House of Correction as "clean, healthy and secure", and remarked that the prisoners performed their work in silence, the men picking oakum and making door-mats and clothes pegs, and the women sewing, washing and picking oakum.

The House of Correction was closed in 1852 after the opening of the new county prison at Wandsworth. The building then became a temporary barracks for the 3rd Surrey Militia until new barracks were built in Kings Road in 1874/5.

48. A watermen's regatta at Thameside (then known as Water-side) in the 1880s. In the foreground are Gridley Miskin's timber barges. On the right is Gridley Miskin's timber store and chimney. Adjacent is Eastland's boat house and, on the corner of Water Lane, the Outrigger pub (rebuilt in 1927). Then comes Turk's boatyard.

By the River

It is often remarked that Kingston has always turned its back on the river. This is incorrect. For centuries the Thames and its Hogsmill tributary were central to Kingston's economic life, with many of the town's principal buildings fronting the water, not backing on to it, as commonly believed. These included breweries, maltings, factories, mills, wharves, boatyards, a tannery and a distillery, many of which survived well into the twentieth century. Furthermore, throughout the nineteenth century, and much of the twentieth, the river was also the hub of Kingston's social life. Because of the Thames, Kingston was for centuries a busy inland port, serving as the main connection to western Sussex and central Surrey. Goods sent from London to Kingston by boat, completed their journey by road. Conversely, goods sent

49. Seacoal was shipped into Kingston for centuries. Palmer's worked their Kingston wharves from 1869 to the 1960s.

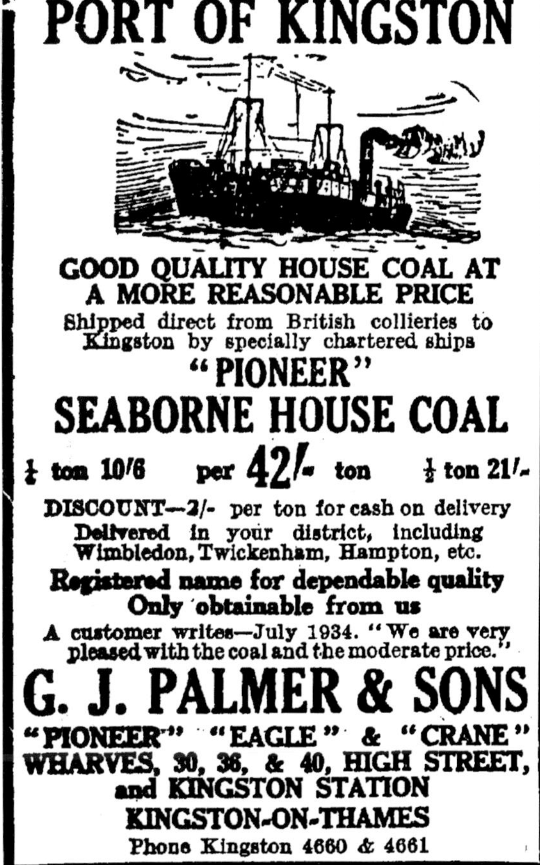

50. A photograph of the 1870s, showing the southern end of High Street from the river. All the buildings have long since disappeared, and the waterfront is now an extension of Queen's Promenade.

51. Town End Wharf, as drawn by H.C. Fox in 1902. It provided public facilities for the handling of cargoes to and from the town's factories. Since 1975 it has been part of the public riverside walk.

52. This painting of the 1950s shows Kingston in its final years as a wharving centre. On the far left is Gridley Miskin's timber yard, with huge tree trunks piled above the roof. Resting near the yard are four of the high funneled tugs used to move barges laden with coal, timber, wheat and tan. In the foreground is the canopied pleasure boat, King Edward. An old-time pleasure steamer passes under Kingston Bridge, while an electric tram passes over it. The flagpole belongs to Eastland's boatyard. Turk's are in the right foreground.

by road to Kingston, went on by barge to London. In a charter granted by Charles I in 1628, Kingston is described as "a very ancient and populous town situated on the banks of the celebrated and navigable river Thames... from which town, by means of that river, different goods and merchandizes, laden in wherries and boats, are daily transported backwards and forward to our city of London and the adjacent parts."

Timber was an important part of this wharving industry, wood from the fine Surrey forests being brought to Kingston for shipment to London. In 1259, for example, large quantities of oak were bought at Kingston for building the Palace of Westminster; and much of the timber for the world-famous hammerbeam roof of Westminster Hall came from Kingston in the fourteenth century. It is also likely that wine from La Reole, near Bordeaux, was being imported direct to Kingston in the thirteenth and fourteenth centuries. Malt from Kingston's many malthouses was sent downstream to London and, from the seventeenth century, the heavy barges returned to Kingston laden with 'seacoal' shipped into London from the North. Good supplies of bark, and the proximity of the river, had led to a prosperous tanning industry by the fifteenth century. Other thriving riverside industries included pottery manufacture, gin distilling and ale and beer brewing, using locally produced malt and hops.

53. Kingston Brewery yard in the 1890s.

Bucolic Kingston

A TOWN OF BREWERIES

There used to be breweries galore in Kingston and so many public houses – one to about 50 residents in some areas – that men frequently challenged each other to walk down any street, have a drink in each pub they passed, and still be sober at the end. It was a challenge many took up, but few could win.

In medieval times ale was consumed at the rate of at least a gallon a day per head of the population. With tea and coffee as yet unknown, milk seized upon for butter and cheesemaking, and no water on tap, ale was the only drink most people knew, and it was regarded as a vital necessity. Thus there were stringent rules on its making, which was mainly the province of women known as ale-wives. Then, ale meant a sweet, thick blend of malt and water, with no additives. Each time a fresh brew was made for sale, the brewer would tie a branch to the end of a pole and hang it outside the house. This was a signal to the local ale-conner: new ale could not be sold until he had visited. Kingston had two ale-conners, important officials appointed by the Corporation, and bound by a solemn oath when appointed. Their job was to taste new ale for strength and purity, and for this they often used their bottoms as well as their mouths. First they tasted the ale, then they would pour some on a bench and sit in it. If their leather breeches stuck to the seat when they tried to rise, the ale was a good one. If they did not, it was judged too weak, and the ale-wife could have her licence suspended or, in extreme cases, she could be wheeled around the Market Place in a barrow before being ducked in the Thames from the town's ducking stool.

Late in the fifteenth century, hops began to be imported from Flanders for the sizable Flemish population living in London, and the English had their first taste of beer. They did not like it. The sixteenth-century dietician, Andrew Borde, declared: "Specyally it kylleth them the which be troubled with the colyke and the stone and the strangulion; for the drynke is a cold drynke; yet it doth make a man fat, and doth inflate the bely, as it dothe appeare by the Dutche mens faces and belyes." This distaste was eventually broken down and beer became even more popular than ale. Also, unlike ale, it kept longer, so could be brewed on an industrial scale.

In Kingston, one of the first to realise its business potential was John Rowle, alias Staunton, a man who found prosperity through the new opportunities opened up during the Tudor age. He is first described as a woodbroker, and is known to have owned several sites in the heavily wooded Coombe district of Kingston. He also had wharves on the Thames, close to Kingston's twelfth century Clattern Bridge and, no doubt, from these he shipped timber from his woodland to supply the great building boom of the sixteenth century. A clue to Rowle's business acumen occurs in documents of 1580, concerning the acquisition of "the beer brew house by John Rowle alias Staunton wood broker of Kingston". The reference to *the* beer brew house is significant, for it indicates that this was the first brewery in Kingston and the foundation of an industry that became the town's main source of wealth for centuries to come. It also

54. Kingston's last surviving malthouse building was at the top of High Street. It dated from the early seventeenth century and was owned by Hodgson's Brewery until 1895, when it was bought by William Smelt and converted into an antique furniture shop. For the next seventy years it was one of Kingston's best loved landmarks, attracting many artists and photographers. Its conspicuous kiln top – a feature from its malting days – gave special character to the street. In 1965 it was given a preservation order, but only six weeks later there was public outrage when it was illegally demolished. Now, a large office block stands on the site.

55. Victorian draymen line up outside the Kingston Brewery in Brook Street ready for the day's deliveries.

indicates that, having sold off his trees, John Rowle used the land to grow hops for the popular new 'bere'. This is also suggested by the names of some of his lands, such as Great Hoppyngs, Hoppyngs, Middle Hoppyngs and North Hoppyngs (remembered in today's Hoppingwood Avenue). Many Flemings arrived in Kingston during the Tudor period, and are noted in local archive documents as 'aliens' or 'Dutchmen'. There is, for example, mention of "Godsall, bere brewer and Dutchman" in 1548.

Several industries allied to brewing grew up, such as coopering. These were initially based in Bittoms Lane and West-by-Thames, the ancient thoroughfare that was renamed High Street in the nineteenth century, and which at one time had eleven breweries.

There were several reasons why Kingston was so active in malting and brewing. One was the river, which provided the large quantities of water required, and made the town an important inland port when barges were the only means of industrial transport. The Kingston area had thousands of acres under cultivation, so much of the barley needed for malting, and the hops required for beer, could be grown locally. Other factors in Kingston's favour included its market and its position on the main London to Portsmouth Road, both of which ensured a great many travellers and visitors who patronised the numerous inns in the town.

But the coming of the railways killed Kingston's malting trade. In 1837 – the year before the London & Southampton Railway Co. opened the first stretch of its line from London to Woking – the town had 38 flourishing malthouses. Three years later, seventeen had closed and the rest faced ruin. "The river had given facilities to the Kingston maltsters which the inland traders of Surrey could not possess; but now the rail took the malt from distant towns to the London market at lower rates than the bargemaster. The diminution of trade was so great that in the spring of 1840 there were seventeen large malthouses vacant in the town", recalled Frederick Merryweather, a one-time editor of the *Surrey Comet*.

HODGSON'S BREWERY

By the end of the Victorian era, all the malthouses had closed. Brewing, however, continued well into the twentieth century, and of Kingston's many breweries, four stand out; Nightingale's, East's, Fricker's and Hodgson's.

Hodgson's was the oldest and biggest. It occupied an extensive site in Brook Street, taking its water from the Hogsmill River which flowed through its grounds, and was reputed to have been in continuous opera-

56. Fricker's Eagle Brewery – an early photograph taken from the river.

tion for more than 300 years when brewing finally ceased in 1951. Earlier it had been owned by the Rowlls family. They occupied Kingston Hall, a Georgian mansion which stood in parkland adjoining the brewery. In 1854, when the Kingston Hall estate had been demolished to make way for St James's Road, the brewery and its ninety tied pubs were acquired by William Hodgson, a brilliant workaholic who had arrived in London a few years previously with only a single sovereign in his pocket. By 1900 Hodgson's Kingston Brewery was one of Britain's major breweries, with 130 tied houses. It occupied the west side of Brook Street, and included its own farriers, coopers, blacksmiths and wheelwrights, together with a malthouse. Close by was a large stable block for the three dozen or so horses who pulled Hodgson's red and gold delivery drays and vans all over Surrey.

In 1943 the brewery was acquired by Courage, but in 1951, because of the growing popularity of bottled beer, Courage ceased brewing there, and gave the premises over to bottling. The brewery closed in 1965 and, after years of planning blight, was finally destroyed by fire in 1971. Now its site is covered by shops, offices and a multi-storey car park.

OTHER BREWERS

Fricker's Eagle Brewery was a fine, towered building on Eagle Wharf, behind Kingston High Street. It was founded by Thomas Fricker early in the nineteenth century, and subsequently passed to his son, Arthur. But Arthur died suddenly at the age of 37, and the business was run by trustees during the minority of his children. In 1903, despite bitter protests from the Fricker family, the trustees sold it to Hodgson's, who paid the large sum of £121,280 to buy out their biggest local rival. Hodgson's ran the Eagle Brewery for a few years, but their main interest was the acquisition of Fricker's 38 tied houses. Brewing on the site ceased, and the wharf was used by coal barges instead. But the brewery's Eagle Tap survived as a pub until 1965, when magistrates ordered its closure because there were seventeen pubs within a half-mile radius. The building is now converted into shops.

George Nightingale established his Kingston Brewery in about 1830. It was on the north side of Pheasant Lane (later renamed Vicarage Road), with another frontage to Water Lane. Early in the 1860s, Mr Nightingale built a new brewery on the opposite side of Pheasant Lane, equipped with the latest steam-driven plant and noted among connoisseurs as Nightingale's Steam Brewery. It was specially known for its Sovereign Ale, which won international awards.

The premises were bought by Kingston Corporation in 1891 and demolished to make way for the town's first council-built housing. Today the site is covered by the John Lewis department store. But three of Nightingale's four pubs still survive: the Six Bells in Albert Road, the Grey Horse in Richmond Road and the Castle in King Charles Road.

East's Albion and Star Brewery was owned by Kingston's first nonconformist mayor, Joseph East. Until 1867 it occupied a building in Church Street that had been a brewery since Tudor times. Then it was transferred to new, purpose-built quarters in Oil Mill Lane (now Villiers Road). Shortly before Joseph East's death in 1891, this brewery was bought by Charrington's. In 1905 they sold it to Vine Products, who operated Europe's largest winery there until 1989. The site was redeveloped for housing in 1996.

57. The only known photograph of Kingston Distillery, where Kingston Gin was made to a secret recipe until 1925.

58. A delivery van from Whitbread's bottling plant in Kingston. The house in the background is now a block of retirement flats.

DISTILLERS

Kingston's long association with alcohol included spirits. There was a distillery south of Bishop's Hall, off Thames Street, from the late eighteenth to the mid-nineteenth century. Rating assessments also show a distillery in the area of West-by-Thames – the former name of High Street – run by the Stevens family for most of the eighteenth century and into the early years of the nineteenth. This may have been the same business that operated alongside the Creek and Clattern Bridge from 1790 to 1925. In 1886 this firm, then called Kingston Distillery, was acquired by its former manager, Edward Coppinger, a prominent town councillor. He retained it until his retirement in 1919, when he sold out to Messrs Searle Gordon.

Kingston Distillery closed in 1925 and was auctioned as "a well equipped rectifying and compounding gin distillery, enjoying the distinction of having the only rectifier's licence south of the Thames." The sale also included Creek House, Mr Coppinger's fine Georgian residence adjoining the distillery. Both buildings were bought for redevelopment as shops. Since 1968 the site has been occupied by Kingston Police Station.

WHITBREAD'S

Kingston's links with liquor were further strengthened in 1901, when Whitbread's opened a bottling plant in Ceres Road (later re-named Wood Street). The beer was brought there from Whitbread's London breweryby bonded carmen in red horse-drawn vans. The bottling was done by gangs of seven, who each had to bottle nine butts (648 dozen pints) per day.

In 1975 Bob Ford, a 90-year-old former employee, remembered life at Whitbread's. "The plant would be working flat out from 6am to 6pm, and people used to say they didn't make a living. They merely existed... That was true. The gangs' wages were pitiful, ranging from 3s 6d (17.5p) to 15s (75p) a week. They were all supplied with macintosh aprons and wooden clogs, and the men were allowed a ration of free ale. I've never forgotten the Christmas week of 1904, when we achieved a record at the Ceres Road depot. We sold no fewer than 10,000 dozen pints in seven days!" The plant bottled Family Ale, London Stout, London Cooper and India Pale Ale. This was delivered all over Surrey in chocolate coloured horse vans supplied by William West, a local contractor.

Mr Ford also remembered when Whitbread's produced dinner ale and stout at 4d (approximately 1.5p) a quart. Before the quart bottle, they had sold beer in jars, retailing at 1s 4d (approximately 6.5p) per gallon. Whitbread's premises were acquired by Bentalls in 1970 and demolished in 1987 for the building of Bentalls new department store.

59. The junction of Kingston Market Place and Church Street, painted by J. Wilson in 1869. On the left is the Mitre, later renamed the Criterion, one of the first casualties of the campaign to reduce pubs in Kingston. Adjoining it is the former Queen's Head.

LOOSE CONTROL

Drinking in old Kingston was not all beer and skittles. "There were an incredible number of public houses continually resounding with the noise of riot and intemperance", wrote Tobias Smollet in his *History of England*. "They were the haunts of idleness, frauds and rapine, the seminaries of drunkeness, debauchery, extravagance and every vice incident to human nature." He was describing eighteenth-century pub life in and around London, but Kingston was representative of such squalor.

Local magistrates were lax in enforcing the liquor laws. Licences were granted to almost everyone who asked for them – the Horsefair area of Kingston had one licensed house to every 37 people – and restrictions on hours virtually ceased to exist. In 1787 the Home Secretary issued a Royal Proclamation against vice and immorality. The Royal borough, like most others, began tightening up the regulations and restricting the hours. Beer and cider houses could remain open only from 6am to 10pm. On Sundays, Good Friday and other "public fasts or thanksgivings", opening hours were 1pm to 3pm and 5pm to 10pm. The good work was considerably hampered by the Beerhouse Act of 1830, which enabled anyone whose name was on the rate book to open his house as a beer shop. No justices' licence or control was needed – merely a two guinea fee to the Excise. "Incredible orgies occurred, accompanied by gambling, brutal amusements and licentiousness", declared a Parliamentary report of 1833. This state of affairs continued until 1869, when beerhouse licences were brought under the control of magistrates. Today there are several pubs in Kingston which began life as eighteenth and nineteenth century beerhouses.

CULLING THE NUMBERS

The big guns of the temperance movement were trained upon the pubs of Kingston throughout the early 1900s. In 1903, for example, Kingston Temperance Union sent one of its chief officers out with a watch and a pair of stout boots to pace out the trail of liquor trade outlets in the town centre. His report shocked members. Starting from Kingston Station, he passed ten pubs in 4½ minutes. From the old Blue Anchor in Thames Street he went by sixteen pubs in eight minutes. A few days later, the Association for the Promotion of Public Morality waited on Kingston Council to demand a reduction of licences in the Royal borough. There was, they had calculated, one licence to every 315 of the population, including women and children. They kept up the pressure, and slowly their influence prevailed until, in 1910, they had the triumph of seeing two pubs closed down in the Market Place.

There was good reason for their zeal. One of the most shocking facts of life at that time was the prevalence of *delirium tremens* among children. Youngsters of thirteen were allowed to drink beer in pubs, while those of sixteen and over could drink spirits. Children under thirteen could – and usually did – go to the local each evening to fetch a jug of beer for the family supper; and it was common to see children at pubs on Sunday mornings queuing for beer to go with the weekly roast. Many took a tipple from their jugs on the way home, and the damage was done. Even babies become drunk after being given beer to sip. Publicans were quick to seize on this source of revenue by bribing children with sweets and buns to buy the family supplies from their particular establishment.

More pubs closed in 1912 after Sir William Vincent, chairman of Surrey Sessions, called on magistrates throughout the county to conduct a purge. If they considered any pubs in their area to be redundant, he said, they must not hesitate to send up their licences to the appropriate authority for extinction. Kingston was swift to comply. Within days, the magistrates had selected four licences as redundant. There was shock at two of the names singled out for the axe: the Blue Anchor and the Old Harrow, both focal points of Kingston for centuries. Only two years

60. The Blue Anchor in Thames Street was a favourite haunt of bargees and watermen for two hundred years. This is the last picture before it was converted into Percy Harrison's outfitting shop in 1912.

61. It was a grievous loss to local historians when the sixteenth-century High Street building that had once been the Crane Inn, was demolished in 1954 and replaced by a characterless bank and shops. In its last days, the old building was well known as the Old Curiosity Shop. On the right is part of the Griffin.

previously, two other central pubs (the Criterion and the Coach and Horses, both in the Market Place) had been closed. No wonder serious drinkers felt threatened. The Blue Anchor, known until 1898 as the Anchor, had been a hostelry for some 200 years and was a favourite place of the hundreds of bargees and watermen who came to Kingston when it was a busy inland port. They slept in the attics, whose windows can still be seen today.

Hodgson's Brewery fought hard to save it, but in vain. What defeated them was the fact that in an area of only one eighth of a mile, there were fifteen fully licensed houses, two beerhouses, one on-wine licence and six off-licences. This amounted to one licence to every 72 people, including women and children.

The Blue Anchor was converted into a shop, and much of its original frontage survives in Thames Street. The case against the Blue Anchor applied equally to the Old Harrow, a short distance away in Apple Market. In addition, the magistrates were able to point out scathingly that its rooms were "too low and dingy". That was hardly surprising. The building had been there since about 1500. In fact, its upper floor remains today as the oldest surviving domestic structure known in Kingston. After its demise as a pub the Old Harrow was converted into shops. The upper floor was raised on hoists while the ground floor was rebuilt, and then it was lowered into place again. The result is that the downstairs section is more than four centuries younger than the upstairs!

LOST INNS

It is odd that modern Kingston has no hotel in its centre, for once upon a time there was no place of its size in Britain more lavishly endowed with travellers' accommodation and every building from 2 High Street to 11 Market Place was a residential inn

62. Kingston's oldest surviving pub building is the seventeenth-century Druid's Head in the Market Place. Since this picture, it has been extended into the adjoining premises as a Whitbread's Hogshead Tavern.

63. The Griffin was established in the sixteenth century, and for centuries was an important posting house and the hub of commercial and social life in Kingston. This picture was painted by J.H. Wilson in 1860. Later, the inn underwent many improvements, including the addition of a handsome ballroom much frequented by the nobility and gentry of the area. It closed in 1986 and was converted into shops.

or hotel. They were substantial places too, as shown by Hearth Tax documents of 1664, when this west side of Market Place was known as High Row. Some of the most important people in the land once ate, drank and slept on the spot now known as 2 to 6 High Street. Today it is offices and shops, but four centuries ago it was the Crane, immortalised in State Papers as the inn where ambassadors and members of the Royal Court lodged when the monarch was in residence at Hampton Court Palace. Later, Cromwell established his county military HQ there during the Civil Wars. During the seventeenth century the building was divided, one part becoming cottages and the other remaining a pub. In the next century it was renamed the Bear and in the next the Jolly Butchers, a name it retained until its closure in 1912. The old pub then became a picturesque restaurant known as the Olde English Café and later as Ye Olde Post House. Meanwhile, the rest of the building became the Old Curiosity Shop, run for many years by the Wrathall family. Today such a building would be preserved. Not so in 1954. In that year it was demolished – largely on the grounds that it was not old enough to merit saving. It had been thought to be thirteenth century, but when it was found to be "only" of the late fifteenth and early sixteenth centuries, its fate was sealed.

Next door was the Griffin, long the leading hostelry in town, which began life in the reign of Henry VIII. It was sold for retail redevelopment in 1985, but most of its old frontage has been preserved, and its original coaching entrance is now an attractive little shopping mall, while its fine nineteenth-century ballroom on the first floor is a restaurant.

The Hogshead, adjoining the Griffin at 2 Market Place, was the Swan Inn in the early 1550s, later renamed the Red Lion, and then the Lion. It was an inn until the nineteenth century, when it was converted into a corn and forage shop by Marsh's, the celebrated millers (see p58). In 1996 the premises were acquired by Whitbread's, who have skilfully converted it into an extension of the Druid's Head pub next door. This was a favourite haunt of author

Jerome K. Jerome and retains a fine seventeenth-century staircase and wonderfully preserved seventeenth and early eighteenth century interiors on the upper floors. Today it is the sole survivor of the thirteen hostelries which once stood in Kingston Market Place.

In Tudor times, a substantial inn called the George stood at 4 Market Place. By the early nineteenth century it had become Kingston's general post office. Here came the Portsmouth mail coach at 10 o'clock each night, with the driver in gold and scarlet livery and the guard sounding a horn that brought sight-seers running. Today the National Westminster Bank stands on the site of the George and part of the Castle Inn, which adjoined it.

Two fine inns stood on today's Charter Quay site, at 6 to 9 Market Place. One was the Castle, which flourished in Tudor times. In the seventeenth century it was replaced with what was probably the first brick building ever seen in the town. Early in the eighteenth century it was refronted and modernised for a new career as a noted coaching inn. Next door was the Crown, which was welcoming travellers in the days of Charles I and was an inn until the 1760s. Then it was converted into the factory and shop where the Ranyard family made and sold their famous Kingston Candles. The site of both pubs was later used for a department store, which closed in 1987. It was then earmarked for Charter Quay, a new housing and leisure development. But the inn's ancient cellars still survive below ground.

Next door, Woolworth's stands on the site of what was once the Sun Hotel. It had a 160-foot river frontage and landing stage, popular as the starting point for the Kingston to Oxford pleasure steamers. It also had gardens so splendid that a *Surrey Comet* reporter in 1856 was moved to eulogise: "Extensive views, unequalled by any place between London and Oxford... with the silvery Thames running at the rear, furnished a complete amphitheatre of foliage which cannot fail to excite wonder and admiration. They also combine every facility for boating, fishing and other aquatic amusements... there is also every accommodation for bowls, skittles and other outdoor sports... we are sure that all who visit these gardens will agree in opinion that they are a temple where the goddess Flora has lavishly showered some of her choicest beauties and most lavish perfumes." The Sun, which had twenty bedrooms, was bought by Woolworth's in 1930, and replaced by what was long the foremost store in the firm's British chain. So ended five centuries of history. For there had been an inn on this site as early as 1370, called the Saracen's Head. There was also an inn next door, known as the Dog.

Thus at one point Kingston offered a choice of no fewer than eight comfortable inns on the west side of Market Place and more pubs on the north and east sides. One was the Criterion at number 22 – today, with a modern front and roof extension, a shoe shop. No. 23 Market Place is now a jewellery shop, but in previous centuries it was the Queen's Head (see Ill. 59). In 1738 one of the alewives here was sentenced to be ducked in the river for her bad temper. According to the *Universal Spectator*, "to prove the justice of the court's sentence upon her, on her return from the waterside she fell upon one of her acquaintances, without provocation, with tongue, tooth and nail and, had not the officers interposed, have deserved a second punishment even before she was dry from the first." Fire swept through the building in 1973, destroying clumsy later additions, but revealing much of the original building.

The east side of the Market Place, long known as Cook Row, boasted three pubs. The Coach & Horses at no. 26 was used by barefist fighters as a training base before their public contests on Molesey Hurst. It was closed in 1910. A few doors away was the Wheatsheaf, which dated back to 1600, when it was called the Ship. This pub, a favourite with Charles Dickens, still retains some of its seventeenth-century facade on the upper floors. The last pub in the Market Place was the Magdala at no. 41, built in the 1760s

64. The seventeenth-century Wheatsheaf in Kingston Market Place, where Charles Dickens was a customer. It closed in 1962 and was converted into a shop.

65. The Red Lion in Wood Street, with All Saints Church school visible to the the right. In 1905 it was replaced by a new building which was acquired by Bentalls in 1929 for store extensions.

as an elegant house and shop. In 1869 it became a pub, named to mark the successful storming of Magdala in Abyssinia by a British expeditionary force the previous year. In 1884 it became a shop again, and has remained so ever since.

Hobbs fashion shop at 6/8 Church Street was originally the Rose, an inn and brewhouse opened in the 1520s by William Shale, one of Henry VIII's valets. The Royal court was often in this area and several royal retainers bought properties in Kingston. The building became shops in 1867, but much of its original structure can be seen inside. The shops at 2 and 2a Church Street were once part of the Old Crown, which closed in 1984. The ground floor is modern, but the upper floors have been preserved virtually unchanged since they were built early in the 1600s to replace an earlier inn.

VICTIMS OF THE RELIEF ROAD

Kingston's long-awaited relief road cost the Royal borough dear in cash and environmental terms – not least because more than two decades of planning blight preceded its eventual completion in 1990. It also meant the destruction of five large town centre pubs. The first to go was the Kingston Hotel, compulsorily purchased in 1975. Built by Edwin Wells, a noted local craftsman, and opened opposite Kingston Station in 1879, it was said to be "of noble proportions", with 25 bedrooms, a large assembly room, billiard room, public coffee rooom and – a rare facility then – a coffee room for ladies. It was primarily aimed at travellers using Kingston Station, which had opened sixteen years previously. Oddly, though it enjoyed many years of prosperity, no known photograph of it survives.

Another relief road victim was the Row Barge,

66. The Dolphin pub stood on the Clarence Street/Wood Street corner. In 1936 it was demolished for the widening of Wood Street (to the right in the picture). Neighbouring buildings in Wood Street that also went included the Jubilee Temperance Hotel, All Saints School and the public swimming baths – all visible here. The John Lewis store now covers the site.

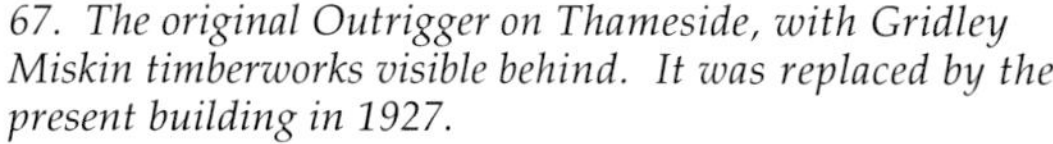

67. The original Outrigger on Thameside, with Gridley Miskin timberworks visible behind. It was replaced by the present building in 1927.

68. The Crown & Thistle at the junction of Thames Street and Clarence Street. It closed in 1962, was converted into a shop, and has since been demolished for offices and shops..

69. The 300-year-old Kings Arms coaching inn in Clarence Street was replaced by this building in 1928. It closed in 1956 and Lloyds Bank now occupies much of the site.

close to the river in Old Bridge Street. This closed in 1982 after a history spanning well over 300 years. Another long history of quaffing ended in 1985 with the closure of the Castle on the corner of Fairfield Road and Fairfield West (now known as Wheatfield Way). The ancient beerhouse here had been rebuilt in 1897, and was much patronised by farmers and stockmen who came to the weekly cattle market that was held in Fairfield West until 1957.

Other pubs lost to the relief road included the Royal Charter in Canbury Place, the Magnet in London Road, and the Jolly Brewer, which disappeared in 1988. The last named had opened in Canbury Passage some 150 years earlier as a modest beerhouse to serve labourers from the surrounding fields and market gardens. It was later rebuilt to serve residents of the terraced houses that soon covered Canbury Fields after the opening of Kingston Station in 1863.

70. The original Three Compasses (shown above) in Eden Street had a history dating back to Tudor times. Its 1906 replacement was demolished in the 1980s to make way for the Eden Walk shopping precinct.

The Millers

The name of Kingston was changed to Kingston-on-Thames in the fourteenth century to distinguish it from Kingston in Yorkshire, which became Kingston-upon-Hull (now simply Hull). It might equally have become Kingston-on-Hogsmill. For this little river, which flows through the heart of the town before joining the Thames just south of the Market Place, was a vital part of the town's economy.

Hogsmill supported eleven watermills between Epsom and Esher, of which five, according to the Domesday Book of 1086, were in Kingston. Exactly where these were is uncertain, but they probably included the three that survived into the twentieth century.

One was Chapel, or Leatherhead Mill, on the site now covered by the Corporation refuse depot. Another was Middle Mill, south of the Fairfield. The third, known variously as Hogs Mill, Hounslow Mill and New Mill was on a site now covered by the apartment block, Edinburgh Court.

In the fourteenth century Chapel Mill belonged to the Lovekyn chantry chapel in Kingston. In the 1770s it was converted into an oil mill, and a fine Georgian house built in the grounds for the owners of this new local industry. Linseed was brought up the Thames in barges to the Kingston wharves, then carried to the mill on carts.

Oil milling made a big impact on this isolated country area, with its fields, farm labourers' cottages and windswept Bonner Hill, where hunstmen in scarlet coats raced behind their hounds. For the rural calm was broken by the incessant noise made by the heavy stompers falling on the linseed – a noise that never stopped from midnight on Sunday to midnight the following Saturday. The mill hands worked a 12-hour shift round the clock, the night shift finishing at midnight on Saturday to start again as the day shift on Monday morning. Meanwhile the fresh night shift began at midnight on Sunday, the duty engineer going in at 10pm to stoke up the fires. The noise of the stompers carried for miles, and people lying sleepless at night would long for the few hours peace that Sunday brought.

In the 1880s, the mill site was acquired by the LSWR for a railway line from Surbiton to Kingston. The line never materialised, and in 1895 the mill was bought by William Smith and converted into a candle factory.

The name of Mill Street marks the route to Middle Mill. By the nineteenth century it had ceased flour production and had become "the only cocoa fibre manufactory in Surrey.". The coarse fibres from the outer shells of coconuts were here made into mats and brushes.

By 1880 this industry had ceased, and Middle Mill and its ten acres were sold to Kelly & Co. the printers and publishers. Kelly's Mill, as it became known, was a valuable source of employment in the town until 1932, when the firm moved to Andover.

The Kingston site was then split between other concerns and Middle Mill as a self-contained community, with its own workers' houses, ceased to exist. The site was redeveloped by Kingston University in the 1990s. Now only the names of two pubs, the Coconut in Mill Street, and the Kelly Arms in Alfred Road, survive as reminders of how people in this area once earned a living.

The third mill to survive into the twentieth century was Hogs Mill, the last Kingston watermill to produce flour. Legend suggests that it was originally owned by a twelfth-century miller called Hog, who gave his name to both mill and river. During the

71. Old Chapel Mill, or Oil Mill.

72. Middle Mill was occupied by printers and publishers, Kelly & Co. from 1880 to 1932. This picture was taken in 1918.

nineteenth century it was always known by the name of its current owners. Thus in the 1830s and '40s it was known as Mercer's Mill, after its then owner and occupier, William Mercer. In the 1870s, it became Marsh's Mill, from the best known of Kingston millers, the Marsh family.

John Marsh had opened a corn chandler's shop in Kingston Market Place in 1814. Eventually the business expanded, under the management of his two nephews, to become one of the most successful firms of its kind in the country. The Market Place premises – now a Hogshead Alehouse – remained its headquarters, but other branches were opened in Wimbledon and Esher. The Marsh family also occupied the famous windmill on Wimbledon Common. In fact they were the last to work it. When they left in 1865, after a dispute with their landlord, Lord Spencer, they prudently took all the stones and machinery with them to deter any newcomers to the building. They then moved into their new Down Hall Mill in what is now Vicarage Road, Kingston. Their main product, Stan-Myln Flour, was so noted for quality that the firm supplied Queen Victoria, Edward VII and George V under Royal Warrant.

Early in the 1870s, the Marsh company took over Hogs Mill, and built up a great reputation as corn, forage, hay and straw merchants. Their yellow delivery vans, pulled by teams of splendid horses, became a familiar sight at many stately homes.

When the two Marsh brothers, each of whom had served two terms as Mayor of Kingston, retired, Hogs Mill was sold in 1896 to Johnston & Co, makers of Yewsabit, a paste, made to a secret formula, and advertised as the 'King of Metal Polishes'. The Johnston company was unswervingly nationalistic. Only English employees were taken on, and its advertising extolled the virtues of buying British and avoiding foreign imports.

73. Hogs Mill after its conversion for the manufacture of Johnston's Yewsabit paste.

74. Production of Yewsabit in the former Hogs Mill.

Yewsabit's finest hour came with the Boer War, when it was putting a shine on most of the British Army. By 1910, however, it had gone. Hogs Mill itself was demolished in 1935 and replaced by the Coronation Swimming Baths.

Marsh's Down Hall Mill closed in 1914 and the firm's premises in Kingston Market Place were acquired by the corn and seed merchants, Thornton and Stimpson. Marsh employees then set up business as coal, coke and forage merchants at 118 London Road, and traded under the name J & B Marsh until about 1950.

Hogs Mill was crucial to many Kingston households during its career as a corn mill. It was the custom, when Kingston was surrounded by wheatfields, for women and children to claim their ancient right to glean the fields after harvest. They gathered up the dropped ears of corn in the stubble and then had to separate the kernels from the husks. They used their feet to do this, putting the corn in their backyards or kitchens and treading on it. Then wheat and chaff were both taken to the nearest open field when a stiff breeze was blowing, and laid out on a cloth. The women would take a plateful from their pile, lift it high, then let it fall. The chaff was carried away on the breeze, leaving the kernels to fall back onto the cloth.

After this the process was repeated hour after hour until the winnowing was complete. Then came the triumphant procession to Hogs Mill, where the hard won kernels were made into flour.

75. Turk's Boatyard c.1872.

Building Boats

THE TURKS

In 1986 the remains of a medieval boatyard were unearthed from the riverside on Kingston's Horsefair site, along with the oak timbers from three thirteenth-century cargo vessels. These boats *could* have been built by members of the Turk family, who claim to have been working on the Thames for at least 800 years – in 1175 they were helping to build two galleys "for the defence of the Realm". They were also ferrymen and fishermen, and in Tudor times kept the fish weir which supplied the Royal table at Hampton Court Palace.

But the family did not become an established business until 1777, when Richard Turk set up his boatyard on the riverside at Kingston. The firm, R.J.Turk & Sons, has remained in Kingston ever since, passing down in an unbroken father-to-son succession.

During the nineteenth century the firm built vessels for Queen Victoria, the German emperor, the King of the Belgians, and many other international Royals and aristocrats. It also built the racing craft used at most of the skiff regattas on the Thames, and the pleasure boats used in London's municipal parks. Author Jerome K. Jerome regularly hired Turk's rowing boats, and his famous *Three Men in a Boat* began their journey from Turk's yard. The firm still builds boats occasionally, but is chiefly engaged in operating pleasure launches and supplying craft to film-makers all over the world.

THE BURGOINES

Kingston was shocked when Alfred Burgoine Ltd went into receivership in 1910; for the firm had played an illustrious part in Kingston's career as a boating centre. The company began in the 1860s, when brothers Charles and Alfred Burgoine set up business on the riverside off High Street. Alfred's genius was revealed when the Thames Sailing Club was born in Kingston in 1870. ("As a builder of yachts which raced under the rules of the Sailing Boat Association, he was supreme," declared his obituary in January 1927.) He also built centre-board gigs. These included *Mona*, the first winner of the challenge cup presented by Queen Victoria to the Upper Thames Sailing Club in 1893, and *Ulva*, which twice won the Queen's Cup. In 1873, he received a Royal Appointment to build Queen Victoria's State Barge, rowed on the Thames by a crew of Queen's Watermen

76. Turk's new Albany Boathouse shortly after it was built in Lower Ham Road in 1896.

77. A Turk advertising blotter of 1914.

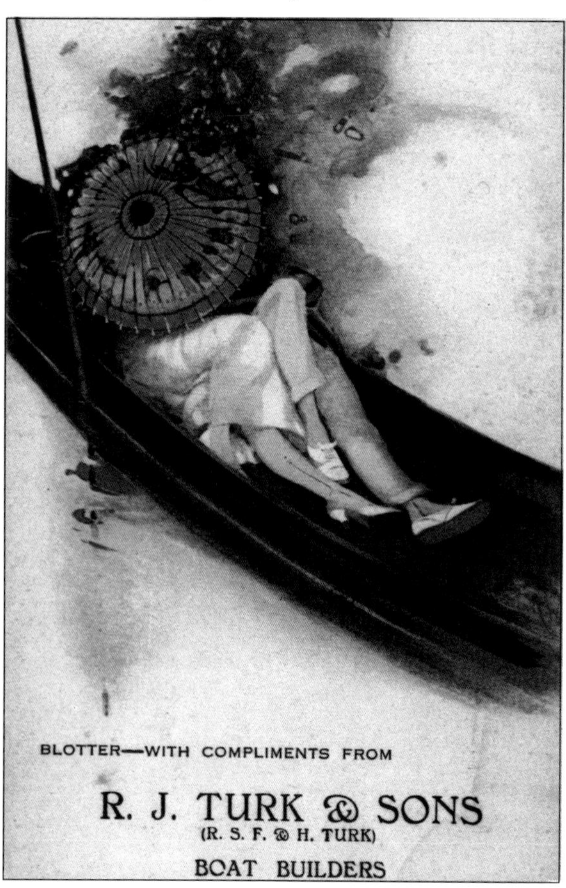

on many ceremonial occasions. This craft is now in the Maritime Museum of Canada in Halifax, Nova Scotia. He also built handsome vessels for Edward VII. Later he was captivated by marine motoring, producing engines that were far ahead of their time. A major triumph for him here was *Maple Leaf*, which attained the then astonishing speed of 65 mph.

Burgoine's brilliance as an engineer and designer was greater than his business skills. His premises at 22 High Street, with a 150-foot frontage, went first, on the order of the Chancery division of the High Court. They were sold in 1910 and became the home of the pioneering aero-engineers, T.W.K. Clarke. Later the site was taken by Boats and Cars – a firm still recalled with fond nostalgia by older residents. Two weeks later came the sale of Burgoine's riverside premises at Hampton Wick. They were acquired by his son-in-law, Harry Offer, who had married his only daughter, Vera, in 1904. Mr Offer formed a new limited company to continue his father-in-law's business.

Burgoine's has long ceased to exist as a boat company. It has evolved into the Offer Group, a name synonymous with building development and estate management, and its Hampton Wick site, redeveloped as offices, is still known as Burgoine Quay.

THE MOULDS AND EASTLANDS

The Moulds, who took to the river in mid-Victorian times, began their business in an unusual way. William Mould was a chimney sweep, who lived in

78. Two bright young things relax in a Burgoine hire boat in 1917.

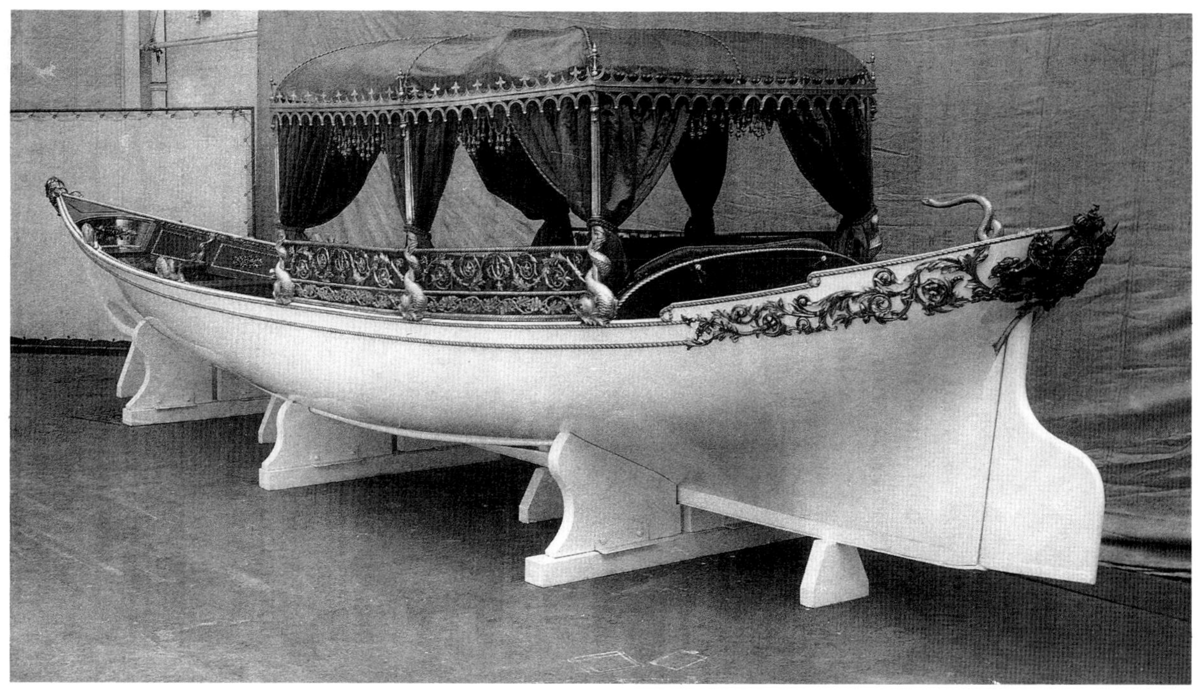

79. Queen Victoria's ceremonial barge built by Burgoine's of Kingston in 1873.

80. Mould's first steam launch, Jessie, photographed in the 1880s.

81. Eastland's Boatyard in the nineteenth century.

a small cottage in London Road. One of his major jobs was cleaning the boilers at Hodgson's Brewery in Brook Street, helped by his son, also named William. The son's heart, however, was set on the river, and when not helping his father, he was building a wooden steam launch on Kingston's public open space, the Fairfield. He called his creation *The Jessie,* in honour of his mother. Then he built a second vessel, named *The William,* in honour of his father. Thus equipped, he set up a boat building and hiring business with his brother, Tom. The two took 39 High Street, the seventeenth-century building that is now a pizza restaurant. They established a boatyard at the back, and they lived with their families in the rooms above. It was here that yet another William Mould was born in 1899. Always known as Bill, it was he and his brother Reg who eventually took over the business and kept it going until their retirement in 1976. Today their moorings and landing stage at Town End Wharf are owned by the Turk company.

The Eastlands were another Kingston boating family who lived and worked on Thames-side for nearly a hundred years. They built skiffs and punts from Honduras mahogany, and hired them out from their landing stage. The Eastlands left the river in 1958, when Len Eastland retired. He recalled when boating was such a competitive business that rival boatmen would go to Kingston Station, touting for hire as day visitors got off the trains.

An unexpected chapter in Kingston's boat-building history came during the Second World War when W.H. Gaze & Son, long known as builders and garden designers, had to take on the new role of building boats for the Admiralty. They built more than 900 vessels, including 150 invasion craft that carried 7,500 men to the beaches of North Africa, Sicily and Normandy, plus fifty water ambulances and hundreds of naval assault craft. The vessels were made in improvised boatyards in High Street by men and women sworn to secrecy. Gaze's own specially designed trailers then took the boats to Town End Wharf, where they were launched into the Thames.

Military Kingston

One of Kingston's most evocative landmarks is a Victorian keep, complete with towers, battlements and a mighty arched gateway, which stands out dramatically in the prim residential architecture of Canbury. It was formerly the entrance to the East Surrey regimental depot and barracks, and from 1875 to 1959 countless thousands of young men marched through it to be trained as soldiers. During the First World War alone, 84,000 voluntary recruits passed through. It was here that a soldier began and finished his service with the regiment; and being the centre of the Old Comrades Association, it was here that reunions and garden parties were held.

Officially, the name 'East Surreys' no longer exists. In 1959, the battalion was merged with the Queen's Royal Surrey Regiment, which in 1992 amalgamated with the Royal Hampshires as the Princess of Wales's Royal Regiment. But in Kingston, the name 'East Surreys' (known as 'Kingston's Own regiment') will never die because it touched so many local lives.

82. A corporal in 'marching order' and a warrant officer in 'undress', drawn at Kingston Barracks c.1895-1900.

83. The dining room at Kingston Barracks in 1913. The two men are presiding over bowls marked SALAD.

84. Kingston Barracks were demolished in 1962 and the site redeveloped as officers' married quarters. But the keep, seen here with its towers, battlements and gateway, was retained as a listed building.

The regiment received the Freedom of the Borough in 1944, giving it the right to march through Kingston "with bayonets fixed, colours flying and drums beating." This privilege was first exercised in 1948, when George VI opened Kingston Power Station, and again in 1952 at a spectacular celebration of the 250th anniversary of the raising of the regiment.

The barracks, built in 1875 on what had been sixteen acres of Lord Liverpool's farm, were redeveloped as army married quarters early in the 1970s. But the keep was retained as a historic monument to a regiment first raised in 1702 to prosecute the War of the Spanish Succession, and originally known as Col. George Villiers' Regiment of Marines.

Six thousand officers and men of the regiment were killed in the 1914-18 war, and 1,196 in the 1939-45 war. The Holy Trinity Chapel in All Saints church, and the memorial gates to the churchyard, are dedicated to their memory.

85. Men at Kingston Barracks in 1913 learning how to cook in the trenches.

86. The Mayor of Kingston, Ald. Gifford Salmon, welcomes home the Volunteer Service Company of the East Surrey Regiment on 8 June, 1901, on their return from service in the South African War.

The Sick and the Poor

EARLY HOSPITALS

Kingston had a hospital as early as the thirteenth century. It was dedicated to St Leonard, and stood in fields outside the town to contain the leprosy that was such a scourge in medieval England. It was granted Royal Letters of Protection in 1217. Then standards began to slide, and in 1315 the lepers rebelled by demolishing the building and making off with the materials.

Kingston's next known hospital opened some 280 years later, and made history as one of the earliest isolation hospitals to be set up by a local authority. Plague was rampant at the time, and the new 'Pesthouse' was so successful in curtailing the epidemic that in 1593 Queen Elizabeth ordered London to follow Kingston's example: "...for we have seen of late an experience in the towne of Kingstone where the infection did begin very hotlie and in restrayninge and keepinge in those that were infected, the same is ceased. They presently upon the fyrste infection, caused an house to be made in the fields dystante from the towne, where the infected might be kept apart and provided for all things convenient for their sustenance and care which, yf so little a town as Kingstone is able to performe, we cannott but thinck that the Cittye of London should... cause some fitt lodginge to be made in some convenyent place without the cittye where those that are infected might be kept apart...".

The Pesthouse survived more than a century on what is now Dudley Road. Then in 1706, when plague had disappeared, Kingston Corporation sold the site for 20 guineas to help pay for the gilded statue of Queen Anne that is still a famous landmark of Kingston Market Place. The Pesthouse itself was sold to Smith's Gift, one of the town's charities, which reassembled it in the Horse Fair as "a house to imploy the poor to work in".

BADGING THE POOR

About this time Kingston Corporation ordered all paupers in the town to wear sleeve badges bearing

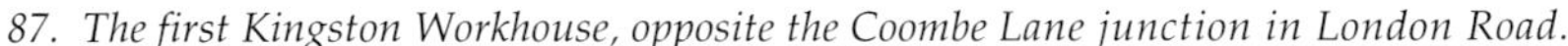

87. The first Kingston Workhouse, opposite the Coombe Lane junction in London Road.

88. The only known picture of the dining room in the casual ward of the Kingston Union Workhouse.

a large red P. Those who refused had their parish relief stopped – as happened to Jeremiah Saunders. He, his wife and their three children had their monthly allowance of 8s stopped because they were "not badged". This was yet another attempt to stem the mounting tide of paupers that were such a burden on the parish. Over the centuries public whippings, the amputation of ears, and even hangings had done nothing to solve the problem.

THE FIRST WORKHOUSE

Eventually, in 1725 the beleagured Kingston vestry prepared a "scheme for the building of a workhouse", stating that as "the poor of Kingston are become very numerous and chargeable it would be advantageous to set up a place where they could be sufficiently maintained and educated and taught to work, read and write, and set to work in order to introduce among the poor habitts of VIRTUE, SOBRIETY, OBEDIENCE and industry and labor, prevent an entail of poverty and idleness and to keep the POOR AT WORK and from begging about the streets and pilfering and other vices AND IDLENESS".

The workhouse began life in a rented building in what is now the Penrhyn Road area of the town, and the rules were strict. Inmates wore a grey uniform and pauper's badge; everyone had their appointed tasks, and lazy workers got no food until their jobs were done. Bad behaviour was punished by three days on bread and water, and if there was still no improvement the culprit was referred to the magistrates, and usually jailed. But the rules also decreed that the house should be run as a "family", with "all possible care to provide peace and good order in the house and treat the elderly people calmly and tenderly".

The workhouse was run by a Master who received an annual sum to maintain the inmates and make a profit for himself. In 1759 Samuel Plummer was paid £420 to provide food, clothes, fuel, medical care and other necessities for the inmates. He also had to pay the rent, provide money for poor apprentices and meet the costs when paupers had to appear before the justices. But he was allowed to set the inmates to work and take the profits. He could also boost his profit by economising on the paupers' food. A typical week's menus of the period show that water gruel, beef broth, pease pottage, bread and beer were the staple items. In 1774 the workhouse was transferred to a seventeenth-century mansion in London Road and there it stayed until, following the Poor Law Amendment Act of 1834, Kingston Union and its board of 21 elected guardians took over in 1836.

89. Sleeping quarters in the Union Workhouse Casual Ward.

THE UNION WORKHOUSE

The Union represented thirteen parishes, namely Hampton, Hampton Wick, Teddington, Kingston, Ham, Hook, Long Ditton, Thames Ditton, Esher, East and West Molesey, Wimbledon and Malden, and it was clear that the old workhouse in London Road was inadequate. So, in 1837, the Guardians paid £750 for five acres in Coombe Lane for the building of a new institution.

The new workhouse was a red brick neo-Tudor building, designed by Charles Luck of Surbiton. It could accommodate 320 paupers, and was handsome enough to be dubbed 'The Grand Palace' by disgruntled local ratepapers. It opened in the summer of 1839, but conditions inside belied the grand exterior. Within weeks there were so many complaints against the Master and Matron, Mr and Mrs William Smith, that the Guardians set up a committee to investigate. They found the Master was using handcuffs, leg irons and "other irons of confinement" to ill-treat the paupers, while his wife was "much wanting in temper and discretion". The Smiths escaped with a reprimand; but the following year they were dismissed.

THE SICK POOR

An interesting feature of life in the new workhouse was the attention paid to the sick. Hitherto, the authorities had sent an apothecary round the parish to visit the sick poor in their homes, while workhouse inmates were often boarded out when ill. Now there was a medical officer to oversee the sick in the workhouse, and gradually to bring about an increased awareness of the importance of good health. Hence the decision in 1843 to have a purpose-built infirmary that laid the foundations for today's Kingston Hospital. Caring for the sick became an ever-increasing part of the workhouse regime – a fact noticed with chagrin by the ratepayers. In January 1868 the *Surrey Comet* noted that of the 344 inmates of 'The Grand

90. The Duchess of Albany visited Kingston Workhouse in 1904 and was photographed with the Matron and nursing staff.

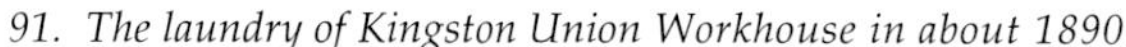

91. The laundry of Kingston Union Workhouse in about 1890.

92. The Workhouse inmates celebrate Queen Victoria's Diamond Jubilee in 1897, with a gala tea in the grounds. The Mayor can be seen in the centre background, resplendent in top hat and civic chain. Women inmates wear white mob caps. To the left are swings provided that day for the children's entertainment. Part of the avenue of limes still survives just inside the Coombe Lane entrance to Kingston Hospital.

Palace', no fewer than 260 were under medical care. "It certainly does seem as if workhouses, as they are called, are fast being converted into infirmaries", the *Comet* remarked. The first infirmary of 1843 was inadequate almost as soon as it was built, patients often having to lie on the floor through lack of space. There were years of what the *Comet* described as "a great amount of talk, a still greater amount of correspondence, many resolutions, counter-resolutions, amendments and rescindings of former resolutions" before a much-needed second infirmary, designed by Charles Luck, was completed in 1868, costing the irritable ratepayers £7,000. This had beds for eighty patients in eight wards "built upon the principle now adopted in modern hospitals with windows on both sides so as to ensure ventilation. They are all lighted with gas, and heated by means of open fireplaces, which serve to add cheerfulness." In the basement was a 'dead house' with what the architect termed "an impervious ceiling to prevent the possibility of

93. The first Kingston Workhouse Infirmary, completed in 1844. This picture was taken shortly before its demolition in the 1980s to make way for a new car park and maternity unit. There was a single-storey building to the left, which originally housed homeless men in casual wards. This was later converted into pathological laboratories and demolished in 1991.

94. The imposing HQ of Kingston Board of Guardians. The building is now Kingston Register Office.

any unpleasant emanations finding their way into the ward above." This infirmary – now used as offices – was soon working to capacity and, despite later extensions, it was clear a third infirmary would be needed.

In 1897 the Guardians embarked on their most ambitious project: the construction of a new male infirmary, nurses' home and porter's lodge, completed in 1899 at a cost of £22,832. The new building had 132 beds and was beautifully equipped for its time, but in 1902 it was separated from the workhouse and called Kingston Infirmary. The medical staff consisted of one resident doctor, working under the direction of a part-time medical officer, to cope with more than a thousand patients a year.

KINGSTON HOSPITAL

Another milestone in the infirmary's history was the First World War, when many beds were reserved for military casualties, and improved surgical equipment was installed to deal with them. The war did much to show how efficient Kingston's Poor Law infirmary could be, and in peacetime it began treating patients from the long waiting lists at general hospitals. The only obstacle was prejudice. The word

95. The second Workhouse Infirmary, built in 1868. It now houses some of Kingston Hospital's administrative offices.

96. *Laying the foundation stone of Kingston Hospital's new nurses home, 1927.*

'infirmary' was inextricably linked with the Poor Law and pauperism, so the Guardians renamed it Kingston and District Hospital in 1920. From then on non-pauper patients were no longer ashamed to go there.

Facilities steadily improved until 1930 when, after nearly a century, Boards of Guardians were abolished and replaced by Public Assistance Committees. The Kingston Guardians mourned the change, but had the satisfaction of knowing that their hospital had been judged the best in the county by the new Public Assistance Committee for Surrey, who renamed it Kingston and County Hospital.

THE CARERS

Keeping a competent nursing staff - or indeed, any nursing staff at all – was a constant problem for the Kingston Union throughout the nineteenth century. The main reasons were low pay, poor living conditions and the often unpleasant and dangerous work when dealing with "lunatics and dangerous idiots". For instance, an unfortunate workhouse nurse in 1840 had to deal with a "pauper female in a paroxysm of lunacy who broke a quantity of windows and did other damage, there being no straitwaistcoat or other means of prevention of similar accidents." By 1897, resignations were so numerous that the Guardians decided they must attract "a better class of nurse". Pay was increased to an annual £33 for charge nurses, £27 for assistant nurses and those attending imbeciles, and £20 for those caring for the infirm. These salaries, it was emphasised, were to include the time-honoured perk of 'beer money'. It was also decided to provide a purpose-built nurses home "where relaxation, quiet and rest can be obtained after hours of duty". This was completed in 1898 with 31 bedrooms and rooms for reading, sitting and dining. The Medical Officers, too, worked hard for little return. In 1897, Dr. Cowen, Medical Officer for the Malden district, complained that his salary had stayed at £40 a year since his appointment in 1886, even though the population of his district had nearly doubled, and in the previous twelve months he had made 1,497 visits and supplied 1,298 medicines. Meanwhile, Dr James Donald, Medical Officer at the workhouse, said he received the same salary as had his predecessor forty years earlier. Yet in that time beds had increased from 50 to 300.

Details of medical treatment given in the Kingston Union infirmaries are hard to come by, but it is clear that beer and wine were considered prime tonics. Nursing mothers were prescribed a pint of beer daily, while port was regularly administered to patients

97. The third Workhouse infirmary, built in 1897 and demolished in 1996. The central tower contained a reserve water tank "at an altitude capable of serving all parts of the house." Later it served as a lift shaft.

until well into the twentieth century. There were no ambulances until 1897. Accident cases were brought in by furniture van, or any other available vehicle, until a Guardian moved that "an ambulance drawn by a horse ought to be at hand for use in such a large Union, and without it we shall be behind the times." His resolution was accepted.

In 1913 Kingston Infirmary had 47 nurses. By 1930, when it was known as Kingston and District Hospital, it had 107. It also had a fine new nurses' home, formally opened in 1928 by the Duchess of York. A visiting reporter enthused over the "jolly bedrooms, fitted with every convenience, and in which any woman could feel thoroughly happy and at home."

REBUILDING

By 1936, plans had been prepared for the complete rebuilding of the hospital; but World War II halted the scheme. In 1948 the National Health Service was born, and the following year the workhouse – prosaically renamed the Central Relief Institution some years previously – was transferred to the Regional Hospital Board, together with the neighbouring Victoria Hospital. The Board thus had the whole of the former Kingston Union site, and began planning its development as an integrated hospital. The main Kingston Union buildings have been replaced by today's ultra-modern structures. But some remain. They include the 1898 nurses' home, now a clinic; the 1868 infirmary, now used as offices; and the Board of Guardians HQ, now Kingston Register Office.

FIGHT FOR THE VICTORIA

The Victoria Hospital was built to commemorate Queen Victoria's Diamond Jubilee. The Duke of Cambridge gave the site – a three-acre field exactly opposite the workhouse – and formally opened the building in 1898 as Kingston's first general hospital. It ran on voluntary donations until the formation of the National Health Service in 1948. The Government then announced it would take over the Victoria, convert it into a gynaecological unit, and run it as part of Kingston Hospital. This autocratic decision sparked rage throughout Kingston. Twenty thousand people signed a protest to Parliament and doctors mounted guard on the building, even barricading themselves inside in a vain bid to stop the takeover. The outcry made national headlines and continued until 1951, when the Victoria's supporters were forced

98. Kingston Victoria Hospital, drawn by its honorary architect, Maj. Henry Macaulay. He was also Kingston's borough surveyor.

99. The Duke of Cambridge (on the left wearing a top hat) opened the Victoria Hospital on 12 December 1898. The building was demolished in 1996, and replaced by flats.

to concede defeat. They vowed to open a new Victoria Hospital, and set up a deed of trust to raise funds. By 1955 they were able to buy Coombe Manor, a detached house less than a mile away from the old hospital. It cost them £10,000, plus £19,000 for conversion work and equipment.

The New Victoria Hospital opened in 1958, and since then has treated well over half a million patients. Initially it was funded by voluntary contributions, but now it is given over entirely to private beds. However, the New Victoria, which is among the top five of Britain's 225 private medical hospitals, has retained its charitable status, and profits are either reinvested in the hospital, or used to provide treatment for the less well-off.

SURBITON HOSPITAL

Surbiton Cottage Hospital in St James's Road made headlines in 1883 as the first purpose-built hospital in what is now the Royal Borough of Kingston. Designed by Edward Carritt, it replaced Surbiton's first hospital, which began in a house in nearby Victoria Road in 1870.

A new Surbiton Hospital superseded it in 1936, but the old building survived a further forty years, first as an annexe to Kingston Hospital and later, under the new name Claremont, as the only hospital in the UK staffed entirely by general practitioners. In 1933 three hundred architects entered a competition for the best design for a new Surbiton Hospital to be built on the site of Hill Manor in Ewell Road. The winner was Wallace Marchment. His single-storey, H-shaped design, ultra-modern for its time, was dubbed 'the suntrap hospital'. The 62-bed hospital cost £54,000, raised by voluntary subscriptions, and was officially opened by the Duchess of Gloucester in July 1936.

THE SCATTERED HOMES

Until the nineteenth century, pauper children were put into Kingston workhouse alongside adults of all ages, backgrounds and conditions. Then, in Victorian times, they were boarded out with cottagers eager for the weekly 4s 6d subsistence fee. Finally, in 1903, the Board of Guardians set up Scattered Homes for the children in their care. These were a series of buildings supported by the poor rate, but intended to give poor children a happy family-style upbringing away from the atmosphere of the workhouse. The main one was at Kingston Road, New Malden. It was divided into four semi-detached residences, each housing fourteen children, with a house mother in charge of each. There was also a crèche for twenty babies with two foster mothers, plus a kindergarten school, and an isolation hospital with ten beds.

By all accounts, the Homes provided very little happiness, and no family life. Muriel Burton, born in Kingston Workhouse in 1909, and soon afterwards sent to the Scattered Home at New Malden, recalled having to get up at 6am when she was three years old, to do her share of the work. "My particular job was to clean all the pot lids, and the steel edges round the kitchen ranges. I had to make them shining and spotless with emery paper", she recalled in 1975. At the age of five she was sent to another of the Kingston Union's Scattered Homes. This was at Teddington and life there, she said, was much the same as at New Malden. "We had to be up at 6am and work before breakfast. Then we changed our clothes to go to school. There was a short and a long route to school, and we were always made to walk the long one. Effort was supposed to be good for us, and we certainly had to make an effort all the time. At midday we came home to dinner, but before eating we had to put on working clothes and do a few jobs. Then we had our meal, changed back into our ordinary clothes, and returned to class. At teatime it was the same again – housework, then tea, then more work, then bed at 7.30 with lights out at once and no talking. For work we wore big aprons made of sacking. The rest of the time we wore the uniform of print dress with black shoes, and stockings held up with elastic garters, which we made ourselves. Underneath we had horrible calico drawers. They came right past our knees and we were only allowed to change them once a week. We seldom sat down except for lessons. All our meals had to be eaten standing up so we couldn't put our elbows on the table, and we had to walk up and down stairs with our arms folded, so our hands wouldn't dirty the banisters. We had dormitories with beds in rows, but no other furniture except a wooden chair to put our clothes on at night. The meals were mostly the same. For breakfast we had bread and dripping. Dinner was usually stewed vegetables. Our tea was bread and marge, with jam on Sundays. We seldom had meat. We never had butter, cake or fruit. To drink we just had cocoa made with water – never any milk or tea. Once a week we were allowed a hot bath, and we had to wash our hair with carbolic soap."

Mrs Burton recalls that much time was spent praying. "On weekdays we prayed before and after meals, and in the evening", she said. "On Sundays we had morning Sunday school at 9am. Then we went to church. Then we went home for dinner. Then we went to the children's afternoon service, then evensong in the evening. After evensong we had to go home and copy out the sermon in our best writing. It was one of the few times we sat down at home."

At the age of fourteen each girl was found a live-in job as a domestic servant. She was in disgrace if she did not stay in her first job for a year, but after that, she was free to take any job she chose. Conditions were a far cry from now. Mrs Burton was paid £1 a week in her first job, with three hours off once a week, plus two hours every other Sunday and a day off once a month.

Surprisingly, she feels no bitterness. "Modern experts would say we workhouse children had a shocking upbringing, but it didn't do us any harm. In fact, those early years have made me appreciate life so much. We learnt that no-one has a divine right to anything, and you must earn things by your own effort. I've met other girls from the Scattered Homes over the years, and they all say the same."

100. Kingston Board of Guardians' home for pauper children in New Malden. The buildings were designed to look like family homes, with four houses each accommodating 14 children. there was also a kindergarten school and an isolation block with ten beds. Today, the buildings are used as a resource centre.

101. Kingston Amateur Regatta off Thames-side, late 1890s.

A Town of Regattas

Kingston had an annual Royal regatta well before the famous event at Henley. It was the Kingston Watermen's Regatta, launched and paid for by Queen Adelaide, consort of William IV, during her residence at Bushy House, just across the river from Kingston. She inaugurated it early in the 1820s (Henley Regatta did not arrive until 1839), and it was held annually on her birthday, 18 August. It was open to everyone employed on the river at Kingston or Hampton Wick.

The first Kingston Amateur Regatta was held on 1 July, 1857 and was, literally, a washout! "Before noon, gathering clouds, accompanied by peals of Heaven's artillery, gave unfortunate indication that the cheering prospects of early dawn would be dissipated," declared the *Surrey Comet*. There was fierce thunder, and the rain came down in torrents throughout the six hours of racing. Nevertheless, participants and spectators enjoyed the event enough to continue it in the years that followed. Its base was the Sun Hotel, in Kingston Market Place on the site now occupied by Woolworth's, where a fine riverside garden enabled paying members of the public to watch the programme.

Kingston Rowing Club was born the following year and by 1861 had become large enough to introduce an annual dinner (six courses and a tankard of sherry for 45p); and in 1864 and 1865 it won rowing's great prize: the Grand Challenge Cup at Henley. From that time the club became closely linked with Kingston Amateur Regatta, which transferred its headquarters from the Sun Hotel to the club's premises on Raven's Ait.

Another group then established itself at the Sun Hotel. This was the Kingston Tradesmen's Club, which made its debut in spectacular style in 1864 with a river procession from the Sun Hotel to Hampton Court. Church bells pealed, bunting fluttered and the band of the 3rd Royal Surrey Militia played aboard a decorated barge drawn by horses. Behind came the club members in rowing boats. In 1865 the club changed its name to Kingston Town Rowing Club, and launched its first regatta in September. Four years later, when it had changed its name yet again to the Junior Kingston Rowing Club, it organised the first Thames regatta to feature fireworks and a display of illuminated boats. This was so successful that the idea was copied by clubs throughout Britain, and transformed regattas from a specialist pastime to a hugely popular public entertainment.

The organisers of the Town Regatta, as the Junior Kingston Club's event became known, had a fine sense of showmanship. As well as races, they pro-

102. Kingston Borough Regatta Committee proudly display the winners' trophies. On the left of the gentleman in the top hat is the Kingston Coat and Badge, a much-coveted award competed for annually by watermen's apprentices. The picture is thought to date from 1897.

103. A 1930s outing on board Grand Duchess, a popular launch owned by Short's of Kingston.

104. World-famous playwright and Hollywood screenwriter, R.C. Sherriff, first began writing to raise funds for Kingston Rowing Club, which he captained for several years. As an old boy of Kingston Grammar School, he was also keenly interested in the school's rowing club, and left it a substantial legacy when he died in 1984. He is seen in this picture coaching one of the school eights in 1929, when his play Journey's End first made him a household name.

vided such diversions as re-enactments of naval battles, with illuminated boats and real gunfire. Another popular event was Teddington Reach Regatta, usually the last local regatta of the season, with a course from Teddington Lock to Turk's Albany Boathouse in Kingston: "An agreeable feature of this regatta is that ladies are afforded abundant opportunity of exhibiting their prowess with the sculls, and the fair sex never fail to disinguish themselves," remarked the *Surrey Comet*.

Meanwhile, the Amateur Regatta, though active as ever in boating circles, was lost in gentlemanly obscurity as far as the public was concerned. Thus, when the Town Regatta ceased in 1890, the Mayor of Kingston, Councillor James East, suggested that instead of every rowing club in the area holding its own regatta, all should combine for one big annual event. The idea was enthusiastically taken up by the Junior Kingston Club, the Evelyn Club, the Kingston Institute Club and various rowing groups run by Kingston's schoolboys, postmen, firemen and police. For this was the golden age of rowing, when the river was a major local interest, and families owned a rowing boat much as they do a car today. (Local clergy frequently claimed that the greatest obstacle to their work was not the devil but the river, which lured so many people away from Sunday worship.)

Thus was born Kingston Borough Regatta, held for the first time on 30 July, 1900. Local tradesmen took the rare step of giving their employees a half day, and a good time was had by all: "The usual concomitants of civilisation, which are certain to be found wherever men do congregate, such as ice cream stands, coconut shies and similar popular institutions, were present in strong force," reported the *Kingston and Surbiton News*. "The gardens of the Sun Hotel never looked more charming, and when in the evening they were illuminated with countless coloured fairy lamps, the effect was one that recalled memories of Cremorne in its palmiest days." Mr Thomas Skewes-Cox, MP for the Kingston area, presented a Kingston Coat and Badge to be competed for annually by the Thames Watermen's apprentices in a race from the top of Waterworks Reach to a point just past Raven's Ait. The coat was of handsome blue serge, with collar, waistband and facings of vermil-

105. Kingston's first Lifeboat Carnival, held off the Albany Club grounds on 3 July, 1897. Here, the lifeboat (sent by the National Lifeboat Institution) is about to be launched to 'rescue' passengers from a 'stricken' vessel. Thereafter, the Lifeboat Carnival became a hugely popular annual event in Kingston.

ion and silver thread, and cuffs and epaulettes of blue, lined with red satin. The oval badge was of hallmarked silver, sewn to a pad on the left arm. Surviving examples now have great rarity value. The Borough Regatta continued until after the Second World War. Now only the Kingston Amateur Regatta remains. This is run from the Kingston Rowing Club HQ, which moved from Raven's Ait to Canbury Gardens in 1955, and is noted as the largest club of its kind in the world.

THE STEADFAST

There was also an educational activity on the river. In 1912, the 100-ton brigantine *Steadfast*, built in 1878, was bought to serve as an 'Evening Technical School for the Sea' for the lads of Kingston and the surrounding area. She was moored in the Thames at Queen's Promenade, and her name is pepetuated by the Steadfast Sea Cadets Corps, which still flourishes a few hundred yards downstream at Thameside.

106. The Steadfast at her mooring off Queen's Promenade.

107. The Duchess of Albany being escorted aboard the Steadfast by the Mayor, Cllr C.H. Burge, in August 1913.

108. George VI inspects Steadfast cadets in Kingston in 1948.

Places of Learning

KINGSTON GRAMMAR

Kingston had schools more than 700 years ago. It also had the first known public school in England. The earliest documentary evidence for this dates from 1272, when "Magister Gilbert de Southwelle, rector of the Schools of Kingston", appears as defendant in a law suit. The schools must have been of some quality; for the prefix "Magister" was reserved for the few medieval scholars who had completed a full university course, while the title of rector was an honoured one in thirteenth-century educational circles.

In 1364 the Bishop of Winchester, in whose diocese Kingston then lay, wrote to Canterbury Cathedral Monastery concerning "Hugh of Kingston.... who presides over the Public School there." This is the earliest reference to a public school yet found in this country.

Evidently this school, too, was of a high standard. The Bishop's letter records that Hugh was a native of Kingston "where a school has been accustomed to be kept". He had been given charge of the school, but the almoner at Canterbury was so loath to lose his skills that he had kept some of his belongings in the hope he would return. The Bishop demanded the return of these goods, pointing out that the people of Kingston needed a master for "their boys and others coming to the said town." The school was therefore important enough to attract scholars from outside Kingston, and to tempt headmaster Hugh away from a place that was then one of England's most distinguished centres of learning.

The location of this school is not certain. But it is thought to have been in the Lovekyn Chantry Chapel, endowed by John Lovekyn in 1309, and where Queen Elizabeth founded Kingston's famous grammar school in 1561. There is no conclusive proof of this, but chantry chapels usually provided education, and it is significant that the only surviving seals connected with the Lovekyn Chapel, attached to documents of 1368 and 1376, bear the emblem of St Catherine, patron saint of scholars. As the chapel itself was dedicated to St Mary Magdalene, there seems no reason for having such an emblem unless there was a school there. At any rate, the Kingston Endowed Schools governors were sufficiently convinced of the school's pre-Elizabethan existence to change its title from the Queen Elizabeth School to Kingston Grammar School in 1904.

109. The medieval Lovekyn Chapel, where Kingston Grammar School was born. In latter years it was the school's carpentry workshop until 1991, when it was completely restored and refurbished. It now houses the school's music department, and is also available for public hire. It is unique as the only free-standing chantry chapel building in England to survive the Reformation.

THE TIFFIN SCHOOLS

In 1874 Queen Victoria assented to a scheme by an Endowed Schools Commission to merge the income from eight local bequests, including those of brothers Thomas and John Tiffin, two wealthy seventeenth-century brewers who left money to educate and clothe needy Kingston children. The pooled funds were to help the ailing Grammar School, and to establish two "lower middle class schools" for boys and girls, to be called Tiffin Schools. As a result new buildings for the Grammar School opened opposite the Lovekyn Chapel in London Road in 1878 and the Tiffin Schools opened on the Fairfield in 1880

There were separate sections for 150 girls and 150 boys, and the fees were £3 a year – compared with £10 10s at the grammar school. In 1889 the girls moved to new premises in St James's Road. They moved again in 1937 to a new building in Richmond Road. Meanwhile, the boys' school became seriously

110. The first Tiffin Schools building on Kingston Fairfield. It is now St Joseph's Roman Catholic primary school.

overcrowded. The problem was eventually solved by the purchase of Elmfield, an eighteenth-century mansion in London Road, and the building of a new school in its grounds. This opened in 1929 and has served generations of Tiffinians ever since.

Kingston Grammar School became independent in 1976, while Tiffins are selective grammar schools. All three are officially recognised as among the highest academic achievers in the UK.

Many other schools were established in the nineteenth century. They included Richmond Road School, founded by voluntary subscriptions in 1818 to provide poor children with "elementary education on a sound basis, with religious teaching as found in the Bible." This school, rebuilt by the council in 1907, closed in 1964, when pupils were transferred to the new Rivermead School in Richmond Road. Its old premises are now used by Kingston College.

The Balfour Act of 1902 enabled Kingston, as a borough with more than 10,000 people, to administer its own elementary schools. The first to be launched was Bonner Hill, which opened in Villiers Road in 1906 with buildings and teaching methods far ahead of their time. It flourished until 1980, when it merged with Rivermead under a new name, Tudor School. Tudor closed in 1986, due to falling rolls, and its building was taken by Tiffin Girls, who transferred from their premises next door. The former Tiffin Girls' School is now the North Kingston Centre, home of Kingston's local history research facilities. Bonner Hill has been replaced by housing.

In 1937 the housebuilding boom led Kingston Council to open Latchmere Road School, built for £15,000 to accommodate 400 children aged 5 to 11. "Its purpose is to provide for the new population on the Richmond Park estate, and relieve pressure on the Richmond Road School," reported the *Surrey Comet*. The school still flourishes.

The Kingston churches of All Saints, St Peter, St John, St Luke, St Paul, St Joseph and St Agatha also opened schools. All but the first two are alive and well.

One of Kingston's proudest achievements in more than 700 years of education history was the granting of university status to Kingston Polytechnic in 1992.

Fire and Water

For centuries firefighting was a parish responsibility, and the 'town engine' was kept in the south chancel of Kingston Parish Church until 1815, when parish officers decided to provide Kingston's first fire station. In what was little more than a shed, alongside what is now the Garden of Remembrance, a simple water container on wheels was kept under the eye of a superintendent. There were no firemen, no horses, no alarm system. When fire broke out, as it often did in the heavily timbered buildings of old Kingston, it was a matter of getting together whatever volunteers and horses that happened to be near the engine house. If there were no horses, the engine had to be dragged by hand by volunteers if they were given a constant supply of beer. If the beer ran out, their efforts usually ceased.

That was not surprising. Up to late Victorian days Kingston's water had to be fetched from wells or the river, and fire fighters kept the engines filled from buckets.

In 1833, Parliament empowered councils to levy a special rate for organised fire brigades. But it was another twenty years before Kingston Corporation took over responsibility for fire engines, and even then it was reluctant to spend money. In 1856, when the engine was in a woeful state, it agreed to purchase "eight new lengths of hose and repairs to the value of £2". In 1857, the Corporation seized what seemed an easy solution: it agreed to lend one of the town's two engines to Hodgson's Brewery for a shilling a year on condition Hodgson's kept it fully maintained, made it available to the Corporation when necessary, and provided all the hoses.

By 1870, the borough fire brigade was so inadequate that a group of townspeople decided to set up their own volunteer service. Donations poured in. Soon the new brigade was able to set up headquarters opposite Cleave's Almshouses in London Road and buy one of the first steam fire engines ever used by an English brigade. It arrived in Kingston on 19 November, 1870, and hundreds came to see the wondrous machine, capable of delivering 350 gallons of water a minute. The rebel group called itself the Kingston Volunteer Steam Fire Brigade, and for the next eleven years operated in fierce competition with the official borough brigade. The latter proved unequal to the struggle. In 1881 it disbanded,

111. Kingston Fire Brigade outside their No. 1 fire station in 1910, with their new motor engines.. The building is now a carpet shop.

112. *Kingston Fire Brigade c.1900.*

handing over its rickety equipment to the volunteers. Hampton Wick and New Malden soon followed suit.

In 1887 the volunteers changed their name to Kingston, Surbiton and District Fire Brigade, and opened a new No. 1 fire station at 23 London Road. It was constructed by builder William Lane, one of the brigade's superintendents, who was so devoted to his task that he did much of the work free of charge so that Kingston could have one of the finest fire stations in the south east. Before telecommunications, when fire broke out police notified a team of callboys, who in turn summoned the firemen. Then horses had to be harnessed. The brigade kept two animals at the Jolly Sailors in London Road, and the licensee, James Sumner, acted as brigade horse driver. He would bridle the horses, get to the fire station as fast as he could, and harness them up to the engine. Meanwhile, the hose cart had to be run to the fire by hand. It was cumbersome, filled with the heavy leather hoses of the time, and at the end of the journey the men pulling it were often literally sick with exhaustion. Once at the fire, it took at least ten minutes to get up sufficient steam to work the engine. In 1896 Kingston's first steam engine was replaced by a new model and the next few years saw the introduction of a round-the-clock water supply in the town, plus a horse-drawn fire escape, canvas hose to replace the heavy leather, and instant couplings for the engines.

In 1908, Ald. A. Hall, chairman of the fire brigade sub-committee, suggested that Kingston should replace its steam apparatus with one of the new petrol-driven internal combustion engines. The result was an argument that raged for months. At that time, the brigade had one Shand & Mason steamer, one manual engine, one escape ladder and a single horse carriage. Ald. Hall pointed out that the repayment costs each year of buying two Dennis engines (£212) would be less than that paid out for hiring horses (£230 a year). Kingston Council would not agree. He tried to convince them that a motor could be mobilised in thirty seconds compared with the twenty minutes plus needed for the old one, and could deliver a nozzle capacity of 500 gallons per minute compared with the 350 gallons yielded by the steamer. In vain. "I should be sorry to be in charge of a brigade which had nothing better to rely upon than motors", declared the brigade's chief officer, Mr G.H. Harrison. However, Ald. Hall finally got his way. Kingston's

Littlejohn [Kingston Hide & Co.] [New Malden

EX-TURNCOCK HARRY, OF NEW MALDEN.

Retired, in 1912, after 34 years' service.

The Photographs shew him in the old uniform of the Lambeth Water Co. and modern uniform of the Metropolitan Water Board.

113. At a time when the water supply was turned off each day for set periods, the Lambeth Company employed 'Harry', seen on the left in hisTurncock's uniform of 1878 and right, shortly before his retirement in 1912, in the uniform of the Metropolitan Water Board.

114. Construction of the Lambeth Water Company works at Seething Wells in 1852?

first Dennis motor engine was delivered on 14 January, 1910, and those who had opposed it so vehemently were soon basking in the praise heaped on the town for its pioneer work in the firefighting field. For Kingston was one of the first towns in Britain to use this type of engine. Visitors flocked to the No. 1 station to see it, and many towns sent delegations to report on the new marvel.

Three months later, Kingston's second engine was ready. By coincidence, it arrived twelve hours before the brigade's horse contract was due to expire. The faithful old steamer was sold to Brighton & Hove Gas Company for £120, but before being sent to Sussex by rail it was photographed outside Kingston Library alongside one of the new motors.

By then the No. 1 station was too small and, while wondering what to do about it, the committee was offered a site in Richmond Road for an up-to-date station, plus living accommodation for the permanent firemen. Weekly repayments on land and buildings would come to just under 30s. – the bargain of the century in the view of the committee. The Council, however, rejected the proposal by one vote. And because of that one vote, the building which opened in 1887 to house a small horse-drawn steam engine and a hose cart had to serve as Kingston's fire HQ until 1941. Then, with the advent of the wartime National Fire Service, the brigade at last left its old station to combine with other groups in a large depot set up on the Fairfield. Now the old No. 1 Fire Station is a carpet shop, and the only clues to its past life are the remains of the lookout and hose-drying tower. However, the old fire brigade would be pleased to

115. Opening of the Lambeth Water Company works at Seething Wells in 1852.

know that the brigade *did* eventually get a modern new station – and in Richmond Road, too. But it cost a lot more than 30s. a week. The new building was completed in 1959 for £46,000!

The dousing of fires (not to mention the well-being of residents) was dependent upon an adequate supply of water. For much of the nineteenth century, the supply from the water companies was turned off for several hours each day. If fire broke out after this, the district turncock often had to be called out to turn it on again.

PURE WATER

Lambeth Water Company established a new works at Seething Wells in 1852, and the Chelsea Waterworks Company opened on an adjoining site in 1856. Both companies used Thames water, purified through filter beds, and piped to those residents who could afford it. A good number could not, and went on using water from a gradually more polluted Thames, or from springs and wells in the area. Thus it was hardly surprising that cholera returned to Kingston in 1866. It was not until the 1870s that legislation obliged landlords to instal mains water for their poorer tenants, but often that was only a communal standpipe.

On Wheels

COACHES AND BUSES

The omnibus was introduced into England from France in 1829, when George Shillibeer launched a service along the New Road in London, from Paddington to the City. Until then the monarchs of the road had been stage coaches, long haul and short haul, and the hackney cab.

Kingston's fortunes were closely linked with the long-distance coaches, and more than twenty services used the town as their first staging post in journeys to the south and west. They included such evocative names as the Royal Sussex, Duke of Richmond, Royal William and the Rocket, and they brought prosperity to local inns and traders alike.

There were also local short-stage coaches which, though useful, were expensive and uncomfortable. Travelling by coach involved making reservations in advance. The booking offices were usually pubs – the word 'booking' originated from the fact that every customer's journey was noted down in a special book.

Omnibuses broke new ground by dispensing with booking, and they also allowed a strict timetable, thus greatly reducing travel time. Omnibus companies soon sprang up in Kingston, and there were ugly scenes as firms competed fiercely for custom. This competition continued for the rest of the century, with constant reports of serious assaults between drivers, and of vehicles racing two and three abreast as they tried to run each other off the roads.

TRAMS IN KINGSTON

The 1870 Tramways Act led to rapid expansion of London's horse tramways. Richmond and Kew had services by 1883. But horse trams never reached Kingston. By the 1890s they were being superseded by electric trams, which became a white-hot issue in the Royal Borough. Many felt Kingston should have a scheme run by the American-sponsored London United Tramways (LUT), whose chairman, Sir Clifton Robinson, lived across the river in Garrick Villa in Hampton. Others believed that such an important project, involving the demolition of much property for road widening, should be in the hands of Kingston Council. Feelings ran so high that there was an election in 1900 to settle the issue. In a poll ruined by hundreds of spoiled voting papers, (on which electors had simply scrawled 'No Trams'), the LUT finally won the day.

116. A Tillings horse bus outside the Druid's Head, Kingston Market Place, early this century.

117. *Schoolchildren went in charabancs to the popular Chestnut Sundays in Bushy Park. This is dated 1849.*

118. *The cabmen's shelter at Clattern Bridge in 1897, decorated to mark Queen Victoria's Diamond Jubilee.*

119. Bob – the trace horse kept to help horse-drawn vehicles up Kingston Hill, pictured outside the Albert Hotel in 1914.

On 3 April, 1905, the Mayor of Kingston hacked out the first stone with a pickaxe, and the task of laying the LUT's Surrey lines began at Kingston Road, New Malden. A hundred navvies laid more than 32 miles of track to serve Kingston, Surbiton, New Malden and Long Ditton. It was the largest project of its kind ever undertaken in Britain, and cost around £1 million. It also caused what the *Surrey Comet* described as "complete chaos on almost every hand". Scores of premises came down for street widening, and the *Comet* mourned the loss of "many quaint buildings, cherished memories of a bygone age". But, it added, the scheme was "replete with future possibilities".

There was a trial run of the new service at midnight on 11 February, 1906 when a tram was driven from Hampton Wick across Kingston Bridge into Surrey. Sir Clifton Robinson took the controls so he could be the first man to drive an electric tram over a Thames bridge. The official launch of the service followed on 1 March. Crowds cheered as an inaugural procession of three trams glided over Kingston Bridge, through Clarence Street and London Road, and up Kingston Hill to the terminus at the George & Dragon. Driving the first car was the Mayor, Ald. Henry Minnitt, closely supervised by senior driver, Lewis Bruce. Afterwards, the official party of two hundred gathered for a celebration lunch at Nuthalls Restaurant.

During the battle for the tramways, Sir Clifton had often declared that "trade follows the trams" and predicted that the relatively modest Clarence Street would take over from Thames Street and Market Place as the town's main shopping thoroughfare. He was right.

120. The inauguration of the electric tram system in Kingston by London United Tramways, 1 March 1906.

121. Kingston's first motor bus appeared in 1905, shortly before the electric tramways made the old horse buses redundant. The London & Suburban Omnibus Company was set up by former rival horse bus operators, and this was the first all-British motor bus, built by Crossley-Leyland for 34 passengers.

TROLLEYBUSES

Trams were replaced by trolleybuses from 1931, when London United Tramways became the first trolleybus operator in the London area. The Kingston service began on 15 June, and there was a poignant moment in London Road when the first bus passed the last tram. Two years later London Transport was born, with powers to take over and operate all bus, tram, trolleybus and underground rail services in London and adjacent counties – an area of some 2,000 square miles. The trolleybus heyday was short. Post-war years brought the era of cheap imported diesel fuel, making diesel buses quieter and cleaner than previously, and in 1954 it was announced that trolley buses would be phased out. The last London trolleybus ran from Wimbledon to Fulwell depot on the night of 8/9 May, 1968. Motor buses have reigned supreme ever since.

122. (Above) Outing from the Albion, Fairfield, Kingston, 1919/20.

123. (Below) A 'Diddler' trolleybus.

124. (Right) The last Kingston trolleybus in May 1962.

125. Kingston bus station, built by London General Omnibus Company in 1922 on the former gardens of Canbury Lodge.

126. Norbiton bus garage opened in 1984 after ten years of bitter controversy and a public enquiry. It meant the destruction of a listed building but was described as 'the jewel in the crown of the London bus service'. It was short-lived, closed in 1990 and was demolished soon after.

127. Building Kingston Bypass.

KINGSTON AND CARS

Some of the greatest names in motoring history lived on Kingston Hill during the 1920s and 30s. They included Herbert Austin, who created a sensation with his little Austin 7 car in 1923; Captain Archie Frazer Nash, the sports car pioneer; and Kenelm Lee Guinness, Sir Malcolm Campbell and Henry Segrave, who in turn set new world land speed records. Frazer Nash, Guinness and Segrave were also involved in car production in Kingston. At the same time the Leyland Motor Co. was making its extraordinary Trojan car in Kingston at the factory eventually occupied by British Aerospace.

Another key event was the opening of the Kingston Bypass by the Prime Minister, Stanley Baldwin, in 1927. This road, conceived twenty years earlier, but delayed by the Great War, made history as the first modern bypass road in Britain.

Cars were in the streets of Kingston as early as 1902, and the following year the *Surrey Comet* published a picture of the first local crash. By 1904 car advertisements were appearing in the *Comet*, and in 1907 motor traffic was beginning to outnumber horse-drawn vehicles in central London.

At first it was hoped that motor vehicles, smaller and swifter than horse-drawn ones, would solve the problem of road congestion. But they did not. In 1913 there was a count of vehicles passing a point in Kingston's Portsmouth Road. Twelve years later a census at the same point showed a traffic increase of 125%. This led to the building of the bypass.

MOTOR RACING

Initially, Britain's car makers were far behind those overseas because abroad manufacturers could display the speed and reliability of their models in spectacular road races forbidden in the UK. Then Hugh Locke King created the world's first motor racetrack on 350 acres of his estate at Brooklands, near Weybridge. This put the UK – especially the Kingston area – well to the fore in car racing design. A key figure in those early motor racing days was Kenelm Lee Guinness, who lived on Kingston Hill, and was among the first to race regularly at Brooklands. In 1912 he needed a place to keep his racing cars. He found it in the stables and large cobbled courtyard of the Bald-Faced Stag, a derelict coaching inn at Kingston Vale, only ten miles from Brooklands. He bought the building and spent much time there tuning the engines that made him one of the fastest men in England. As no sparking plug could withstand the heat generated by the engines of his Darracq cars, he designed his own in a machine shop in the inn's cellars. The KLG plug (after his initials) became world famous. It was also used in aircraft production.

128. Kingston's first motor smash.

129. A steam delivery van belonging to Smithers of Kingston

130. A new motor van outside Kingston post office in 1908.

131. *Lankester's new showroom at Eden Street in the 1930s.*

132. *Kenelm Lee Guinness (far left) with his Talbot-Darracq team at the KLG works, Kingston.*

133. A cartoon of 1908, when Kingston justices were noted for their harsh treatment of speeding motorists.

At Brooklands, Guinness met Henry Segrave and Malcolm Campbell, who also lived on Kingston Hill. Between them they gave Britain a golden age of motor racing. During the 1920s they always took the first, second and third places in long-distance events at Brooklands, and in 1922 Guinness set up a world land speed record of 133.75 mph in his modified Sunbeam. Campbell then bought the car and in 1924 and 1925 set speed records of 146.36 and 150.87mph respectively. But Segrave, who had become a manager at Guinness's Kingston Vale works, was not to be outdone. In 1927, driving a specially constructed 1000 hp Sunbeam, he became the first to exceed 200 mph on land, and was acclaimed all over the world. This inspired Campbell to design his Napier-Campbell. Named *Bluebird*, it was built at Kingston Vale, and was so large that a wall had to be demolished to get it out. In February 1928 Campbell broke the speed record at 206.95 mph. Four weeks later, Segrave announced the building of a new super car, with a 900 Napier aero engine and a 235 mph speed. This beautiful car, named *Golden Arrow*, was built at Kingston Vale, and enabled Segrave to raise the world land speed record to 231.36 mph, an achievement which earned him a knighthood.

Another great name of British motoring was Archie Frazer Nash, who produced a legendary range of sports cars at his Kingston factory at 145 London Road, and lived on Kingston Hill until his death in 1965. After the Great War, car manufacturers faced the threat of huge numbers of ex-military vehicles depressing the market for new cars. Leyland, jealous of its good name, bought up all it could, and acquired the former Sopwith Aviation factory in Richmond Road, Kingston as a place to recondition them. "It's weird, but it goes", said designer Leslie Hounsfield of his Trojan utility car, made by Leyland in Kingston from 1923. Its eccentricities included solid tyres which happened to fit standard gauge tram tracks. So if it got into tramlines, it was forced to proceed to the tram depot! Nevertheless, its economical performance made it popular, and at one time the Kingston Works was producing 85 a week. Initially it cost £230, comparable with most other British four-seaters. By 1935 this had dropped to £125, and Leyland claimed that over a distance of 200 miles, travelling in a Trojan was seven pennies a mile cheaper than walking.

Kingston's first motor car crash occurred on Kingston Hill in the early hours of 9 May 1903. The *Surrey Comet* reported: "A party of officers returning to Pirbright Camp after a ball in London, met a three-horse van coming out of Manorgate Road. To prevent collision, the driver of the car, which was proceeding at a great speed, turned abruptly to the right, and then sharply to the left again, at the time applying his brakes so powerfully as to cause both back tyres to burst with a loud report, and the car to swing round on to the pavement and crash into the shop window of Mr. Peter Jamieson's Drapery shop. The car was smashed, and one or two of the occupants seriously injured."

The GN Cyclecar was invented by Archie Frazer-Nash and Ron Godfrey to bring affordable motoring to the masses. Godfrey later teamed up with E. A. Halford and Guy Robins to develop the HRG (famously known as the 'Hurg') and set up HRG Engineering in Oakcroft Road, Tolworth. The Hurg was relatively cheap at £395. It was also fast and reliable, coming second in its class in the Le Mans 24-hour race in 1938, and first the following year. Only 36 had been built when war broke out, and about 200 more were produced post-war. They performed brilliantly at rallies and trials, but production ceased in 1955.

134. *The Trojan utility car, made by Leyland in Kingston from 1923.*

On Rails

THE COMING OF THE RAILWAY

Kingston stayed remarkably unchanged from medieval times to the Victorian age. The Market Place, which was thriving at least as early as 1242, was the trading hub of the town, the main thoroughfares developing round it in a medieval street pattern that survived intact until the massive redevelopments of the 1980s. Industry and housing were concentrated in a small area close to the river and bridge. Beyond that were vast stretches of agricultural and common land, in which places like Surbiton and Malden were mere hamlets.

That began to change after 1834, the year Parliament gave authority for a London to Southampton railway line. It has gone into folklore that Kingston refused to allow the line through its midst because it wanted to protect its coaching trade. So the main line station was sited at Surbiton instead. This story has been much exaggerated. There was indeed some opposition to the London & Southampton Railway Company's original route; but that route did not pass through the town centre and did not include a central station. After Wimbledon, it would have crossed Coombe Lane and Norbiton Common, and continued north of the junction between what are now the Dickerage and Kingston Roads. Then it crossed the Hogsmill and skirted Surbiton Hill. The station that Kingston refused would have been close to the Waggon & Horses at the foot of Surbiton Hill, about a mile from the spot where the station of 'New Kingston' opened in 1838. Initial post-railway development would therefore still have been centred on Surbiton, and the dire effect on Kingston's trade and industry would have been the same.

The railway company seems to have made scant effort to negotiate with Kingston Corporation. It was the opposition of Lord Cottenham, who was loth to have his estate at Wimbledon disturbed, that probably induced them to divert their route. For their policy had been to avoid land whose owners offered opposition. "The line was therefore carried through a barren and desolate country, where the soil was so valueless that landowners were glad to get rid of it at any price", reported a company pamphlet. Cutting through Surbiton Hill, which meant shifting 500,000 cubic yards of clay, was expensive. But it was deemed more economic than treating with intransigent landowers like Cottenham.

136. The railway bridge that carries the line over the Thames from Hampton Wick to Kingston. It was designed by John Errington.

The first Kingston Station was placed deep in a cutting to the west of the present Ewell Road Bridge, and was little more than a hut. "There has been no unnecessary expenses in architectural designs or decorations, the object aimed at having been utility and durability at the smallest possible cost," the Company told shareholders in 1839. The Vauxhall to Woking portion of the line opened in 1838 to coincide with Epsom Races. *The Times* of 31 May reported: "...At an early hour upwards of 5,000 persons were assembled at the gates of the Southampton Railway near Vauxhall for the purpose of going by the railroad trains to Kingston Station, and from thence by other conveyances to the race course. There were ten times more applicants for seats in the train vans than there were seats for their accommo-

135. The first LSWR trains. This drawing was regularly used over their train timetables in the Surrey Comet.

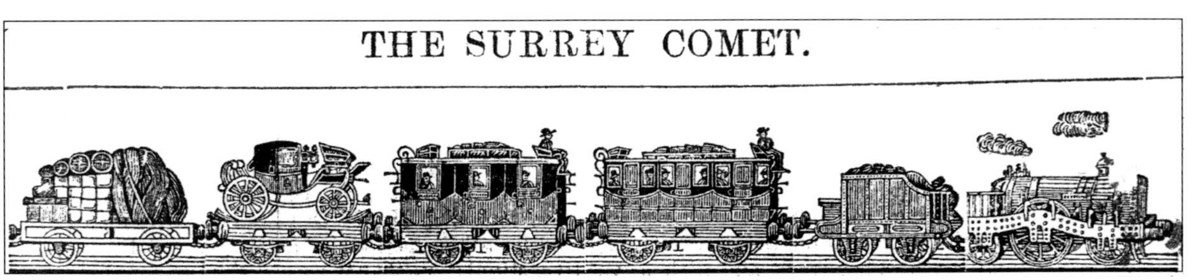

137. Racegoers en route to Epsom Races on the new LSWR trains in May 1838. The picture vividly shows the difference between the 1st, 2nd and 3rd class passengers, and the accommodation they were provided with.

dation. The proprietors did what they could to meet the demands for conveyance, but they could not do what was impossible."

The Company's first timetable had five trains daily each way on the new line, stopping at seven stations. Thirty-one minutes were allowed for the ten miles between Nine Elms and Surbiton at a fare of 3s first-class and 1s 6d second. Journalist Frederick Merryweather vividly described those early trains: "The first-class carriages were low and narrow inside; the luggage was strapped on the roof. The second class were fitted with bare seats and with open, unsashed windows which made umbrellas requisite in rainy weather. The third class ran but once a day, were purposely made as uncomfortable as possible, and were attached to a heavy goods train which shunted at almost every station; they were open trucks with the rudest of benches." He described how the guard sat on the roof, working a primitive brake: "Night or day, through wind or storm, through tunnels and the bleakest country, smothered with smoke or blistered with sparks and dust, the poor guard was often so perished and benumbed as to be unable, when he reached the terminus, to leave his seat without help."

MR POOLEY'S NEW TOWN

In 1839 the London & Southampton Company changed its name to the London & South Western Railway (LSWR). The following year, the 77-mile line from London to Southampton was completed, and in 1848 the London terminus was moved from Nine Elms to Waterloo. Meanwhile, Surbiton's crude little station, reached by a steep descent down the embankment from South Terrace, was replaced by what *The Times* called "a very respectable edifice", opened in 1840 on a site given by the pioneer developer of Surbiton, Thomas Pooley. It was supserseded by the present station in 1938. Described as "a notable engineering and architectural achievement", it is now a listed building.

The opening of Surbiton Station in 1838, and of New Malden Station in 1846, changed local social and economic life for ever as land values rose and new roads and houses emerged on former parks, farms

139. Surbiton Station as rebuilt in 1938.

138. Surbiton Station – built in 1840 to replace the first shed-like structure. The Southampton Hotel, with its pillared entrance, is on the left. The hotel was replaced by an office block in 1960.

140. Kingston's first railway station, opened in 1863.

and commons. The population soared. In 1841, Kingston had 8,094 people. In 1851 the total had risen to 10,630, and in 1861 to 16,123. Initially, development was concentrated on Surbiton, where Thomas Pooley, an illiterate maltster, had bought the 100 acres of Maple Farm; engaged one of the foremost architects of the day, Harvey Elmes; and begun building an elegant new town for "nobility and gentry". But by 1844 Pooley was bankrupt, and Coutts Bank had taken control of his enterprise.

MORE EXPANSION

The influx of new commuters increased after the death in 1850 of Alexander Raphael, who had lived as a semi-recluse in his mansion, Surbiton Hall. Most of its fine parkland, abutting Portsmouth Road and the river, was bought by developer, William Woods, who by 1855 had laid out Surbiton Crescent and the Uxbridge, Anglesea and Palace Roads across Raphael's secluded domain. He also created Grove Road and constructed the first portion of the riverside walk, Queen's Promenade.

The post-railway building boom reached Kingston town itself in 1854, when Charles Rowlls sold his Kingston Brewery, and leased much of his extensive grounds for building. The brewery occupied the west side of Brook Street, and the Rowlls family, which had owned it since 1745, lived on the brewery estate in the eighteenth-century mansion, Kingston Hall. Its grounds included most of the land between the brewery and High Street, stretching south to Oaklea Passage and the Bittoms, with the Hogsmill curving through its groves and lawns. This idyllic scene disappeared after the sale of the brewery to William Hodgson. Kingston Hall was demolished, the meandering Hogsmill stream was straightened, and in 1858 St James's Road was cut through Rowlls Park, with a brick bridge to carry it over the water, and so provide a direct route to Surbiton and its all-important station. Kingston exulted. Trade in the old town had been moribund even before the advent of the railway, and in 1834 a Parliamentary Commission had described the local economy as "stationary". The decline accelerated as the new railway rapidly carried away trades that had been the backbone of the local economy. New roads and houses would bring new residents; and they, it was hoped, would breathe fresh life into dying trade.

In 1856, the *Surrey Comet* noted that "the fields surrounding the town have become so densely crowded with houses that Norbiton and Surbiton far outnumber in population the original town." In September 1859 the paper announced that 3,500 new homes had been built in the neighbourhood; a few months later it was stated that the population of Kingston had nearly doubled since the opening of the station at Surbiton.

141. *Kingston railway station, c.1907.*

142. *Waiting for the 8.10am on New Malden Station in the 1930s.*

143. This 1930s picture recalls an era when Kingston station had a flourishing freight trade. On the left is the goods yard and storage depots. On the right, just beyond the cars, are Fyffe's banana warehouse and sidings. Further on are coal wharves. The goods yard is now covered by an apartment block. All the sites on the right have been swallowed by the relief road, which has an underpass beneath the railway lines.

Kingston was not as desperate for a station as is commonly claimed. Thousands signed a petition of protest when the LSWR announced it would form a short branch line, starting at Twickenham and coming over the river to Kingston via Hampton Wick. Indeed, the *Surrey Comet* remarked on "the opposition the company have uniformly met with at the hands of the majority of townsfolk." Nevertheless, on 19 May, 1861, work began on the new rail embankment on the Kingston side of the river in what had been Goldring's garden in Lower Ham Road (now Skerne Road). The line was carried over the road on an arch before running through the market gardens where the Fitt family had grown rich crops of salad for the London market. Indeed, until the arrival of the railway, market gardens extended south from Canbury Passage to Clarence Street, covering what is now the station approach of Wood Street, and the whole of Fife Road. The station itself was built on the site of what had been one of the largest tithe barns in Britain.

The new line opened in 1863, with fifteen up and thirteen down trains daily to and from Waterloo via Richmond. In 1865 the Kingston Further Extension Act enabled the LSWR to extend to Norbiton and Wimbledon, and further powers were obtained in 1866 to raise the line between Norbiton and Kingston so that it could pass over the London and Richmond roads on arches. This meant considerable alterations to Kingston's attractive little station. It also meant destruction of the Canbury Lodge parklands, the transformation of rural Canbury Lane into densely developed Richmond Road, and the construction of roads and hundreds of houses on what had hitherto been orchards and farmland to the north of the town.

The LSWR's electrification programme began in 1913. The electric service from Waterloo to Kingston, via Richmond, was inaugurated on 30 January, 1916. It offered a train every ten minutes each way between Kingston and Waterloo, with the first each day leaving Kingston at 4.21am on weekdays. Because of the First World War, and the ensuing recession, it was left to the Southern Railway (formed in 1923) to complete the LSWR's electrification project in the 1920s and 30s.

144. *Kingston Tannery workers in the 1930s.*

Malodorous Kingston

THE TANNERS

Old Kingston's industries were as malodorous as many of its inhabitants. The strongest smell came from the tannery, which occupied the old Bishop's Hall site near Kingston Bridge from the late seventeenth century until 1963. It was an important source of local jobs and revenue. Kingston's oak-tanned leather was noted for quality – it was advertised as being the best in the world and much in demand for bespoke footwear. The drawback was the foul smell permanently inflicted on the town by the tannery as it transformed raw, putrefying animal skins into superfine leather. The skins came from local farm cattle, brought to market on the hoof and slaughtered in the town. First, the skins were steeped in lime solution to remove hair and flesh. Then they were placed in pits filled with oak bark and water for a year or more.

Kingston Tannery had 230 pits, plus a beam shed, where hair and flesh were removed; a bark mill shed, where the oak bark was broken and ground; and drying rooms, where the tanned skins were hung to dry. Thus it was a large building, with a river frontage extending from Kingston Bridge to the Bishop's Hall alley. It also employed a large workforce, which not only had arduous and dirty jobs, but whose clothes were so imbued with tanning smells that in the nineteenth century special seats were often set aside for them on horse buses and trams.

The tannery closed in 1963 and a few weeks later was destroyed by fire. Today its site is covered by Bishop's Palace House and part of the riverside walk.

FAMOUS CANDLES

Competing with the tannery for a malodorous reputation was the candle factory on the west side of Kingston Market. It was begun in 1762 by Robert Ranyard, who was succeeded in turn by his son, William, and grandson, Samuel. There was a brisk demand for their goods. Kingston's street lighting consisted of candles set in lanterns, lit each night by a lamplighter who went his rounds with a ladder. Only the wealthy could afford beeswax candles. Everyone else used the rushlights and tallow dips that were a Ranyard speciality.

The Ranyards had a candle shop fronting the Market Place, with workshops behind. Theirs was a picturesque trade, little changed since Roman times. But it had its unpleasant side. For tallow was made by melting down hard fat from offal and mutton, result-

145. *Smith's soap and candle factory.*

ing in what diarist John Evelyn described as "horrid stinks, nidirous and unwholesome smells."

Ranyard's Kingston Tallows were of cotton wick, dipped repeatedly into vats of molten fat. Their rushlights were made from the rushes that flourished on Kingston's river banks and aits. These were peeled, bleached and dried, then dipped in scalding grease. The best were more than two feet long, and burned for an hour.

Samuel Ranyard retired in 1857, and the firm was acquired by his manager, James Smith. He developed the Kingston Sperm Candle, which was made from oil taken from the head cavity of the sperm whale, and became nationally famous. But it was his son, James, who made the firm a major enterprise. He acquired a long established candle factory in Staines, and by 1895 had so increased turnover that he could buy the disused Kingston Oil Mill, on the bank of the Hogsmill river off Oil Mill Lane – since renamed Villiers Road. Here he was producing forty tons of candles a week by 1901, many made from paraffin wax imported in cakes from Burma and America and refined by machinery powered with water from the Hogsmill. Meanwhile, vast numbers of his 'stearin' variety were exported to hot countries because they could withstand fierce sunlight without bending.

Smith also pioneeered several soaps. The most famous was his patented Kingston Volvolutum, said to shift dirt from clothes without rubbing. Smith ran his firm until well into his seventies. In 1920 he decided to retire, but died soon after, and in 1923, Kingston Corporation acquired the site for a refuse depot.

THE SEWAGE AFFAIR

Kingston's rankest and most unexpected industry was born of its nineteenth century sewage problem, which made history as one of the toughest battles ever fought by a local authority. It took many years and thousands of pounds before Kingston Council could announce, with unintended humour, that it had "got to the bottom of the problem" at last.

It all began in the 1860s, when sewage disposal had become a serious problem. There were foul open sewers all over Kingston, and in even the most genteel roads Kingston's medical officer, Mr Kent, reported that the smell from privies was "all but unbearable". The Act for the Improvement of Towns obliged corporations to replace their old systems of cesspools and open ditches by underground sewers. These, it was decreed, must either flow into a convenient river, or be collected on sewage farms.

In 1862, Kingston Corporation organised a public competition for the best drainage scheme. The winner was a Mr Despard, and work began on constructing his project for eight miles of sewers emptying into the Thames. It was halted by the Thames Conservators, who took court action to prevent Kingston from disgorging sewage into the river because it would be "an injurious nuisance". After a long hearing, resulting in 2,500 printed pages and much national publicity, judgment went to Kingston in June 1865. The work was almost complete when, in 1867, came catastrophic news: London's four million inhabitants were to take most of their water from the Thames, and in future no sewage was to be discharged above the capital. This unexpected decision affected towns on a 140-mile stretch of river. Most had only recently been obliged by law to spend huge sums diverting their sewage into the Thames. Now they were being forced, at even greater cost, to take it out again. Resentment was increased by the fact that London itself would still continue to disgorge sewage into the river, but any town up-river which did so would be fined £100 a day.

Kingston Corporation decided to drain sewage into a stretch of porous soil at Ham, then part of the Kingston parish. A host of objectors appeared, the Government rejected the proposals, and the Corporation had to impose an extra rate on its householders to pay the huge costs of the inquiry. Kingston then made another attempt. Determined not to be beaten by the opposition of landowners, it bought 100 acres near Apps Court at Molesey and arranged for Surbiton and Hampton Wick to send their sewage there as well. Again there was an inquiry, again objectors appeared, again the Government refused permission and again the ratepayers had to pay up – not only for an abortive inquiry, but also for the now useless land at Apps Court.

At length, the eminent engineer, Sir Joseph Bazalgette, proposed a scheme in which all the towns in the Thames Valley would take their sewage to Bagshot. There was a public meeting at Kingston to launch the scheme, but again opposition and failure.

After ten more years of fruitless effort Surbiton, backed by Kingston, tried to get legal sanction to form a joint sewerage board comprising every town in the Thames Valley between Windsor and London. The sewage would be removed from the Thames above London and sent to an outfall near the sea. This scheme too failed to obtain permission.

The Thames Conservators, silent all this time, suddenly reappeared to demand huge penalties against all the offending towns. Their wrath fell first on Hampton Wick, which was sued for £98,000, though the whole rateable value of the village was only £11,000. The village's local board, faced with the seizure and sale of their area to pay the penalties, appealed for permission to form a joint board of communities between Hampton and London. There was fierce dissent, but for the first time a local authority

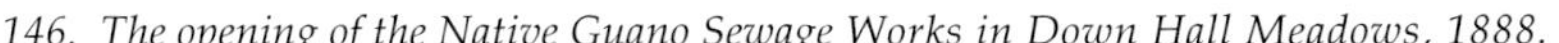

146. The opening of the Native Guano Sewage Works in Down Hall Meadows, 1888.

147. The Native Guano sewage works at Down Hall Meadows, Kingston.

won, and Parliament agreed to a joint board comprising 45 square miles of territory, and three years in which to sort out its sewage. In the meantime, all penalties were suspended.

It seemed that light had dawned at last, and Kingston joined its neighbours in sending its most influential men to sit on the Board: "A stronger band probably never sat down to make their lives wretched over local affairs", commented the chairman, Sir Thomas Nelson. The Board met for the first time in 1877 and wrote to every engineer of note in the land for advice. They got back 23 schemes and appointed an engineer to analyse them all. One was chosen, and work about to begin, when they learned that they needed to obtain an Act of Parliament to proceed. "Next to contests about religion, there is nothing which waxes so warm as a sewage fight", commented Sir Thomas.

After much uproar, 294 objectors out of a population of 110,000 managed to get the Bill rejected. So the Board was unable to carry out its scheme in the three years allowed, and by 1880 members found themselves threatened by more than £1 million in penalties, plus long terms in jail. Sir Thomas sent an anguished letter to the Prime Minister, Benjamin Disraeli. He headed it 'An Incredible Story' and, it is said, put the Prime Minister off his breakfast!

Meanwhile, Kingston, disenchanted with the Board, tried and failed in a host of different schemes. One was to set up sewage farms, and many a mangold and turnip was produced at public meetings to show what fine results the system could produce. Sewage disposal became the topic of the day, occupying newspaper columns year after year and forming the chief topic of conversation at social gatherings. As local journalist, Frederick Merryweather, put it: "at every luncheon or public dinner, the delectable sewage question came in with the dessert." In 1885 the desperate Corporation began negotiations with the Native Guano Co., which opened sewage works in Down Hall Meadows in 1888. Mayors from many British towns, together with journalists from more than sixty newspapers, were invited to see machines, made by Willans and Robinson of Thames Ditton, work with a special chemical to separate sewage into a clear liquid, pure enough to go into the Thames, and a firm sludge that was dried, ground into powder, and sold as fertiliser.

Kingston Corporation said it was "flushed with victory" because their problems had been solved for a mere 1.5 pence in the pound for the building of the works, and 3d in the pound for the sewage treatment. It was a blessing, too, for Hampton Wick, which was soon shooting its sewage to the works over the nearby railway bridge by means of a Shane`s ejector.

148. Kingston 'B' Power Station taking shape on the former sewage works site in 1947.

It was a piquantly appealing thought that the sewage from 35,000 residents of Kingston should be elevated to the status of a British export, prized by growers and agriculturists throughout the world. Townspeople talked proudly of their part in producing bumper harvests in Singapore, and increasing the growth of sugar in Barbados – just two of the places where hundreds of tons of Native Guano were sent from Kingston each year.

Alas, Kingston's fragrant honeymoon with the Native Guano Co. did not last. As the population grew, so did the processing problems. In 1975, 90-year-old George Ford recalled how in his youth the sewage was baked in giant ovens: "There used to be elegant band concerts given from the bandstand on Canbury gardens, and huge crowds would gather on summer evenings", he said. "Sometimes we would hear a clanging noise from the Native Guano works. That meant they were opening the oven doors, and the stench was so great that everyone would flee, leaving the band to play on alone as best it could."

Finally the stench from the sludge-drying process so permeated the town that the Corporation terminated its agreement in 1909. The Native Guano Co. moved to Southall, and paid Kingston two shillings a ton to send its sludge to them by barge for conversion into the rich brown granules so prized by gardeners.

Native Guano continued to be an important Kingston commodity until the sewage works was obliged to leave Down Hall Meadows in 1944 to make way for a new power station. This posed a problem. The Hogsmill Valley Joint Sewerage Board had been formed in 1940, and four years later acquired 91 acres of farmland in Lower Marsh Road for a new treatment works to serve the boroughs of Kingston, Surbiton, New Malden and part of Epsom. What could Kingston do with its sewage in the meantime? Middlesex County Council came to the rescue by taking sewage from Kingston at their Mogden works through a temporary pumping main laid over the Thames. The first sod of the new Lower Marsh Lane works was turned in 1953, and the project was officially opened in 1957 in what had been the fields of Brook Farm. After more than a century, Kingston's sewage problem had been solved at last.

149. The Surrey Comet's workforce in 1888. The building in the background housed the press. Next to it is the boiler and engine room. In the foreground is the composing department.

Tale of a *Comet*

The *Surrey Comet* was born on 5 August, 1854 in the Surbiton house where Thomas Philpott had his home and printing business. Two things made it unique. One was its name – it was the only paper in Britain called the *Comet*. The other was that it was launched by Divine command. For Mr Philpott, a devout Christian, was convinced that God wanted him to establish a paper that would, as he confided to his family, "expose the bad and promote the good".

His backers had more worldly reasons for investing in the new venture. One was that the stamp duty that had weighed so heavily on newspapers since 1712 was clearly on its way out. Because of that, no fewer than 86 provincial papers were launched that year.

Another factor was that 1854 saw the increasingly strong movement for the reform of the old Kingston Corporation, and mounting agitation for independent government in Surbiton. It was a good time to launch a paper in a town that had previously relied on posters, handbills and word of mouth for local news.

The infant *Comet* was laboriously produced on an iron-framed hand press with a slate bed. The first issue cost a penny and consisted of four pages, It could not claim to be a NEWSpaper – that would have meant paying a penny a copy in stamp duty; so it confined itself to comment, general information and the advertising needed to sustain it.

"It will adopt whatever is reasonable and good in the suggestions of all Parties, and endeavour to promote harmony and good feeling where there are contending opinions, as there can be no greater Curse to a Parish, a County or a Nation than strife among those who govern", wrote Philpott.

Stamp duty on newspapers was abolished in 1855, and the *Comet* could at last promote itself as a newspaper. The price rose to twopence, but readers got twenty pages.

Philpott acted as editor, publisher and printer, in addition to running his bookselling, stationery and commercial printing business and doing much voluntary Christian work. With so much to do his health began to fail and in 1859, when circulation had risen to 1,000 per week, he sold the *Comet* to Russell Knapp for £200. Knapp was a dynamic young man of 28, who had trained as a compositor at *The Times*. He moved the *Comet* to a modest shop at 17 Clarence Street, close to Kingston Bridge, and transformed it

150. The composing room of the Surrey Comet in 1909.

into a broadsheet – which it remained for the next 135 years. (It became a tabloid again in 1994.)

Russell Knapp promised "a marked improvement in the quantity and quality of general views". Circulation increased, and in 1863 he could afford to move to a former butcher's shop and slaughteryard at 20 Clarence Street. He invested in new equipment. In 1860 he had bought an iron-framed hand-pulled press. Two years later he installed the *Comet's* first cylinder press which, though hand operated, was a great step forward. Then came a bold move to steam power. Initially it was a failure that cost him dear. But on 23 March 1867, the *Comet* was printed by steam power for the first time, its 6,000 copies run off at the rate of 1,500 per hour. It was still set by hand until 1896, when the *Comet* bought its first Linotype – a machine which did the work of four hand compositors.

Knapp died at the early age of 36, and Mary Anne, his widow, was left with eight children, two of them twins born a month after his death. Courageously she took control of the business and ran it as sole proprietor for 33 years.

Meanwhile, William Drewett, the *Comet's* erstwhile editor, established the *Kingston & Surbiton News* in 1881, and made it a flourishing rival. This rivalry ended in 1900, when Mrs Knapp and Mr Drewett merged their businesses to form Knapp Drewett and Sons. The company continued until 1982, when it was acquired by Argus Press. By then, molten metal had been superseded by computer typesetting.

The *Comet* was bought by Reed Regional Newspapers in 1993, who in turn sold it to Newsquest, a management buyout group in 1996. To date, it has never missed an issue in its 143 years.

151. *The Surrey Comet's home – formerly a butcher's shop and slaughteryard – in 1888.*

At the Polls

The word 'parlement' was first used in England in 1275 to denote a great council between the King and representatives of his people. However, the first Parliament in the modern sense of the word is generally held to be the one summoned by Edward I in 1295. There is no evidence that Kingston was represented at either gathering. But it was soon recognised as a Parliamentary borough in its own right, and regularly received writs to send representatives to wherever 'Parlement' happened to be meeting. In August 1311, for example, Kingston sent Adam Le Templer and Johannes de Cruice to the Black Friars in London. In November of the same year, Rogerus Le Taverner and Johannes Touly were despatched to Westminster. In March 1313 Johannes Touly was again chosen to represent Kingston, accompanied by Johannes atte Crouch

It is known that Kingston selected two MPs in 1335, but there is no record of their names. Then, in 1373, Hugo Taverner and Johannes Haveryng were returned by Kingston to seats at Westminster. After that, the official Parliamentary returns are blank as far as the Kingston is concerned, and it is more than five centuries before the borough appears again as an electoral area. It seems that Kingston cared nothing for the privilege of being a Parliamentary constituency, and had no desire to return its own MPs. Indeed, in the 1370s the townsmen begged leave to be excused the responsibility altogether. They also refused to contribute towards the expenses of the 'Knights of the Shire', as the county MPs were known. By today's standards, this was an extraordinary attitude. But to a medieval borough it made sense: it was not obliged to pay its representatives their daily fee.

In any case, townsmen were loth to serve in Parliament, no matter what the pay. Roads were in an appalling state and most journeys had to be made on horseback. This was significant in that Parliament met in whatever place happened to be most convenient to the King. Thus between 1295 and 1681, when the last Parliament away from Westminster was held, 51 of 194 Parliaments met in different towns.

Having finally reached Parliament after a tortuous journey, the troubles of a town's representatives were by no means over; for the great feudal nobles regarded the so-called 'faithful Commons' as vastly inferior, and MPs often went in peril of their lives.

How did Kingston escape its electoral responsibilites with such ease? Clearly the town, important since Saxon times, was able to influence the Sheriff of Surrey, who was responsible for the issuing of the King's Writ to attend Parliament. Kingston thus withdrew into self-imposed electoral obscurity.

Until the 1830s, Surrey had only two MPs. electors had to travel to Guildford to vote and the poll remained opened for up to a fortnight. Hustings were often violent and noisy occasions. It was not uncommon for would-be voters to be carried off forcibly and locked up until the election was over. Often supporters of one party would beat off voters from the rival faction, or hire mobs to surround hostile electors and cut them off from polling booths. Party agents canvassed Kingston with bulging money bags, and voters could often name their price – provided they were willing to risk a broken jaw when they reached the hustings. The reforms of 1832 did something to cleanse the electoral system, though the vivid excitement remained.

The Reform Act divided Surrey into East and West divisions, each with two MPs. Kingston was a polling place for the East division, and to it came voters from The Dittons, Ham, Hook, Malden, Petersham and Richmond. The run-up to an election was always colourful. Images of hated opponents were burned at the stake, insulting posters were pasted on every wall, and there were daily processions and tableaux.

The hustings were beneath the Town Hall in Kingston Market Place. The Tory headquarters were at the Griffin, an old Market Place inn decked out with bunting in the orange and purple then the Conservative colours. Their Liberal oponents used the Sun (the site of Woolworth's) heavily embellished with the distinctive Liberal blue. As the carriages, laden with voters and paid for by the candidates, arrived in town they were escorted to the poll by the committees of their respective parties, plus two rival brass bands. Each voter had to mount the hustings and publicly answer the question: "For whom do you vote?" The answer, given loud enough for all to hear, was then noted down by the clerk. The voter would leave the poll to the jeers and threats of those who disapproved of his answer, but fortified by thoughts of the feast to come from his grateful patrons. Once elected, the two winners were girt with the sword as Knights of the Shire. A fine sword, believed to be one of those used at the ceremony, now forms part of Kingston's Borough Regalia.

The Ballot Act of 1872, which made voting secret, robbed elections of their entertainment value. However, the formation of Surrey County Council in 1889 restored some of the ginger to local politics. Until then, Surrey had been administered by county magistrates, an exclusive clique usually appointed for life, and not answerable to the people. County councillors were elected by the ratepayers: "The position will be an honourable one, and carry with it a corresponding importance and influence which will make a seat a thing to be desired in itself, irrespective of the inward satisfaction which public service should bring to every well-ordered mind," said the *Surrey Comet* in September 1888. Public opinion was therefore outraged when Alfred Higgs, a Kingston shopkeeper, had the temerity to join the gentry as a candidate. "We can scarcely credit that Mr Higgs is so puffed up by vanity... as to imagine himself a fitting representative of the town on the county council", declared the *Comet*. The townspeople agreed. An effigy of the presumptuous Mr Higgs was mounted on a cart and dragged through the town amid hoots of derision, and on election day he came bottom of the poll.

The next burning topic was where the seat of the new county council should be. Guildford, Epsom, Reigate, Wimbledon, Little Bookham and Kingston were in contention for the honour before Kingston was declared the county town, and County Hall was built in Grove Road at a cost of £43,494. The road was later renamed Penrhyn Road in honour of the Council's first chairman, E.H. Leycester-Penrhyn.

Borough elections are comparatively recent in Kingston. Until 1835, the town had for centuries been governed by a Court of Assembly, led by two bailiffs – the equivalent of today's mayors. This Court elected its own members, and the townspeople had no say. Even so, passions often flared at election time. The most dramatic example was after the downfall of Charles I, when a Roundhead minority managed to seize control of the Court, led by Theophilus Colcock who, with his fellow Bailiff Obadiah Wickes, set out to appoint his own friends and relations to key positions and build up a despotic personal power in the borough. Contemporaries described Colcock as "the most prowd, malicious, insolent hippocrite that ever came into any corporacion, and the most destructive of the corporacion that was ever heard of. He broke wilfully his oath [as Bailiff] and slighted as nothing all the ancient orders, elections, customs and ordinances of the towne to compasse his wicked designes, trampling them as dust under his feet at his pleasure when occasion was offered."

After a break of more than 500 years, Kingston regained its status as a Parliamentary constituency in time for the General Election of 1918. This was the most dramatic the country had ever seen. For the first time women were allowed to vote, all polls took place on the same day, and the counting of votes was delayed for a fortnight to allow returns to be sent in from Britain's armed forces at home and abroad. It was an odd time to embark on the upheaval of a general election. The First World War was still in horrible spate: food was rationed; and the *Surrey Comet* each week carried long lists of local men killed, wounded or captured while on active service. But it was also the year Parliament had passed the Representation of the People Act. This enfranchised women for the first time (but only those aged thirty

152. Norman Lamont during his term as Chancellor of the Exchequer.

and over) and simplified the qualifications for men, so adding thirteen million voters to the register. This new electorate was pressing for a chance to cast its hard-won votes and it got its way.

Polling took place on 14 December, a month after the end of the War, in what has gone into history as the 'Khaki Election'. Kingston had three candidates: J G.D. Campbell (Conservative), who lived in Tankerville, an elegant house on Kingston Hill; Arnold Ely (Liberal), whose father had founded the well-known Ely's department store in Wimbledon; and Thomas Dumper of Tolworth, Kingston's first-ever Labour candidate. Campbell topped the poll with 13,596 votes, trailed by Dumper with 2,325 and Ely with 2,052. But Mr Dumper had the satisfaction of knowing that he and his fledgling Labour party had achieved more votes than the Liberals, who had reigned supreme in Kingston until the late nineteenth century.

Four more MPs, all Conservative, have represented Kingston since: Frederick Penny, from 1922 until his elevation to the peerage as Lord Marchwood in 1927; Admiral Sir Percy Royds, who served until 1945; John Boyd Carpenter, returned at eight general elections before his resignation in 1972; and Norman Lamont, who became Britain's youngest MP two days after his 30th birthday. He was returned in six general elections before the shock announcement in 1993 that Kingston would no longer have its own MP. Instead the Royal borough was divided between the new constituencies of Kingston & Surbiton and Richmond Park.

In the Swim

A FLOATING POOL

Portsmouth Road became a stylish address from the 1850s as developers built mansions and villas of a modern opulence never seen in Kingston before. But newcomers to the town found it had a particularly unsavoury feature: its people stank! Thus it was for hygiene as much as natation that John Dixon, the brilliant engineer who designed China's first railway and brought Cleopatra's Needle to Britain, began campaigning for swimming baths.

The only concession Kingston Corporation had ever made to swimming was in 1872 when, after complaints about nude bathing near Kingston Bridge, they took a seven-year lease on Steven's Ait, put up a canvas screen, and called it 'the bathing place'. It was of limited use. For one thing it was barred to women and girls. For another, the depth and current made it suitable only for strong swimmers. When the lease expired in 1879, the Royal borough was left with no designated bathing facilities of any kind.

Few houses could boast a bath, and those that did were lucky to have water. Even fifty years after the construction of two major waterworks in Portsmouth Road, thousands of local households still relied on pumps and wells, and there was no continuous supply to those fortunate enough to have taps.

So it was a significant improvement when, in 1891, Lambeth Waterworks announced that their water service in the upper part of Kingston would operate from 5am to 9am in winter and 6pm and 8pm in summer.

Councillor Van der Pant, an eminent local dentist, joined John Dixon in the campaign for public baths, pointing out at a council meeting in 1880 that the poor were supplied with coal, soup and blankets, "but no means of being cleanly". And, he added, it was not only the poor who never bathed: "Every class is suffering from this omission, especially ladies, who aren't allowed to swim except under cover." Eventually Kingston Corporation agreed to a swimming bath but, at a time when neighbouring towns like Richmond were spending £5,000 and more on such facilities, refused to part with more than £1,000. It took all Dixon's ingenuity to mastermind a pool for such a meagre sum. He did it by means of a 'floating bath', built on the shore at Lower Ham Road by a local craftsman called James Lobb. It was towed upriver to Kingston Bridge, where Dixon had designed it to be approached by steps from the parapet. Thames Conservators refused to let it stay there, so it was towed to Town End Wharf, and officially opened by the Mayor on 31 July, 1882. John Dixon described it as "a pontoon with a bath in the shape of a grating suspended in the middle, providing the facility of bathing on the top stratum of the river without stirring up the mud and sediment by treading

153. 'Boats and Cars' operated from 22 High Street during the 1920s and early 1930s, providing the first mixed open-air bathing facilities in the borough. These included a large raft in the river for sunbathing and diving, and on-shore changing rooms. There were plenty of boats for hire and "lock-up garages for your cars or cycle while you boat or bathe."

on it." The grating could be raised or lowered at will to provide shallow bathing for women and children, and deep water for men and boys.

Admission charges were 4d between 10am and 4pm, but only 1d from 4pm to dusk. "These prices bring it within reach of the poorest inhabitants, and there is every reason to hope that the venture will not only give an impetus to the extension of the practice of swimming, but will promote habits of cleanliness among the lower orders of the people", remarked the *Surrey Comet*. It added reassuringly: "The promoters claim that bathing establishments of this description are superior to shore baths, which although professedly filled every day, are often filthy and stinking holes, infinitely worse than the river."

BATTLE ON THE THAMES

Meanwhile the Corporation was congratulating itself that its floating masterpiece would be free of rates, taxes and water charges. Then the Thames Conservators intervened: the floating pool must be moved down-river to the tannery, or they would remove it by force. The Corporation refused, saying this was the most stinking and objectionable site in the whole of Kingston. Thereupon the Conservators despatched the steamer *Queen* to Kingston under the command of a Mr Little. Accompanying it was a fleet of smaller boats filled with navvies armed with iron bars. Their aim was to detach the pool from its mooring chains and take it to the tannery. But they reckoned without Kingston Council. Massed on the platform were the town's leading civic dignitaries, each armed with a 20-foot pole shod with iron. With them was a regiment of hastily mustered corporation workmen. The river was running fast that day, and as the invaders reached the platform, the defenders shoved them off with their poles. This went on for two hours, and in the melée Mr Little managed to clamber on to the platform where the borough surveyor, Captain Henry McCaulay, was in charge, while the deputy Mayor, Ald. Frederick Gould, roared more orders from the shore. There was a violent struggle in which blood was spilled, dignity bruised and insults hurled. Finally one of the Conservators aimed a hitcher at Ald. Gould. It caught in his trousers, ripping them from his legs and causing unpleasant injuries. This stripping away of civic dignity was too much for the police squad who had been lying in wait in South Lane. They sprang forward, the Conservators took to their boats and made off, shaking their fists. By then a huge crowd had gathered on the shore and a roar of delight went up as the invaders were routed.

The *Surrey Comet* reported acidly in its next edition

154. The stone-laying ceremony at Wood Street Baths on 31 March, 1897. This picture caused some excitement. "We think this is about the best specimen of outdoor photography with so many living subjects that we have seen," commented the Kingston & Surbiton News.

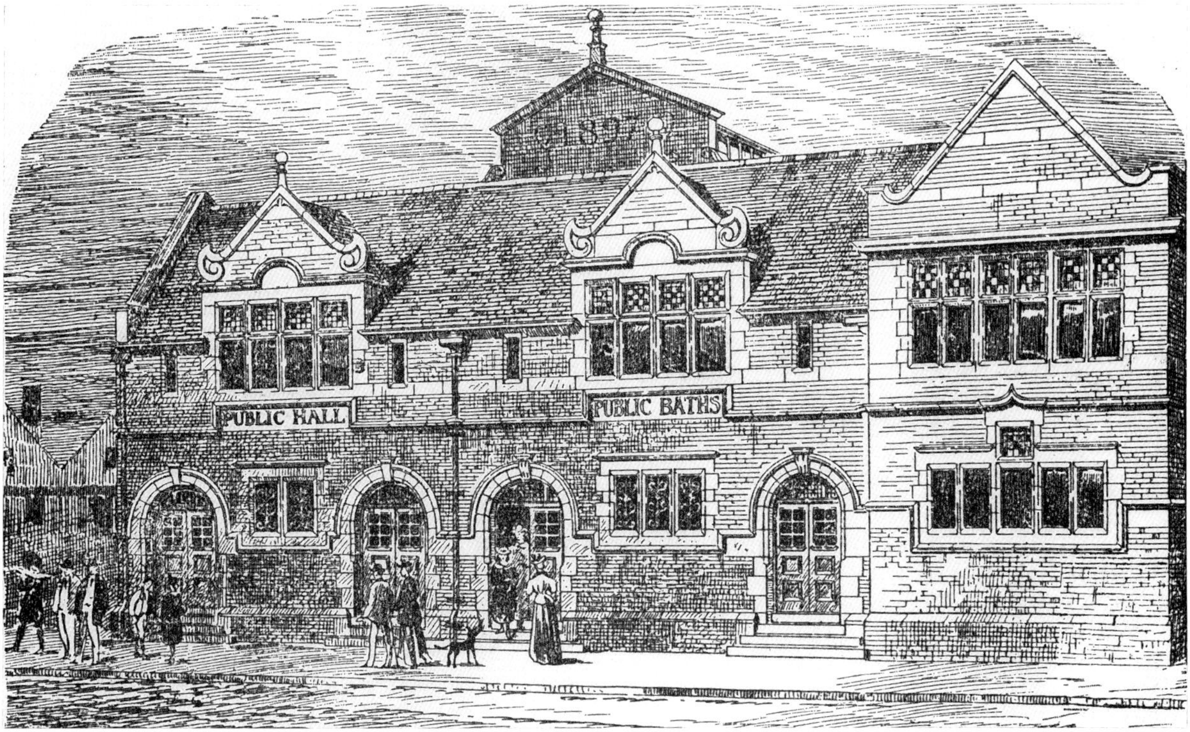

155. An architect's sketch of Kingston's first public baths, which opened in Wood Street in 1897. The competition for the best plan was won by Messrs Francis J. Smith and Maurice B. Adams.

156. The Wood Street Baths on opening day in 1897. Standing on the side are Cllr Homersham, and the chairman of the Baths Committee, Alderman Coppinger.

on "scenes such as have never before been witnessed in Kingston, and scenes which were certainly a scandal to those who provoked them." The Conservators sued the council for assault. But the case was dismissed, and the floating bath stayed put for the next fifteen years. Mixed bathing was forbidden, but the bath was "set aside for females" three days a week. The superintendent was David Pamplin, and his article on bathing and hygiene in the *Kingston and Surbiton News* of 24 May, 1884, spelled out the home truths of Kingston's washing habits – or lack of. "Some still bear the almost indelible marks of their long neglect, but in the course of a few weeks the cleaning will have ceased, offering the bather time to attend more closely to the exercise of swimming", he wrote. "Most after bathing do not dry their bodies, but put clothes straight on. Others use bits of dirty linen, pieces of rag, old socks or pocket handkerchiefs of various hues and degrees of dirt. Therefore I strenuously advise the loan of a towel and bathing drawers for the entrance charge of one penny." Mr Pamplin added that dirt was not confined to the lower orders. "Some enthusiasm has set in (and not too soon) among the upper classes in favour of cleanliness, and one is pleased to see it descending, though its progress is not as rapid as might be wished."

A NEW POOL

John Dixon had wanted a pool that would last for generations. Thwarted by Kingston Council's parsimony, he knew his cut-price floating bath would not last long. By 1890 it was in such a rusty state that Kingston Council, belatedly regretting its meanness in not providing a permanent structure in the first place, organised a competition for the design of a cheap replacement. The prizes were so small that there were only five entries, and the Council asked the two winners to amalgamate their ideas, trim them to the bone and produce the lowest possible costing. The two men came up with a quote of £4,435 for a fine building. The Council eagerly accepted. But before work could begin the men announced they had made a mistake. They should have quoted £8,400. An enraged Council told them to "lock up their plans and throw the key to the bottom of the river", and decided not to bother with new baths after all.

The Council was forced to re-think in 1894, when the disintegrating floating pool was removed. In 1896 a town meeting was called to discuss what had become a highly controversial issue. Councillor Coppinger, chairman of the Baths Committee, pointed out that of 6,127 houses in the borough, 4,346 were without a bath. After bitter controversy, a replacement eventually opened in Wood Street in October 1897, with a 90-foot pool and 27 slipper baths. These were intended to serve the town for the next hundred years, but soon proved inadequate because of the Council's parsimony. The same fate befell their successor, the Coronation Baths. After much delay and financial paring, these opened in Denmark Road in 1936, soon after the coronation of George VI. They were officially opened by the Mayor, Councillor Alfred Dryland, who revealed some misgivings: "It does not do to prophesy in regard to buildings of this type, particularly when we remember that the foundation stone of the baths which these supersede was laid only forty years ago", he declared. How right he was. The Coronation Baths closed on safety grounds in 1980. Four years later they were replaced by the Kingfisher Pool, adjoining Kingston Museum.

The poor state of public hygiene prompted Frederick Gould, William Walter and Samuel Baker in 1855 to convert the town's former debtors' prison into a public bath house. They advertised "warm baths for the poor at 4d each", plus "every description of baths, hot and cold, plunge, shower and medicated", and offered to send portable baths to all parts of the town. The venture failed. "We could not get people to come and have a bath, even if we gave them tickets for nothing", mourned Ald. Gould. The premises, after which Bath Passage is named, closed in 1862. In 1897 the council decided to alter the building "so as to render it available for public lavatory and urinal purposes". It was demolished in 1934 to make way for the new Guildhall, but new conveniences were built in Bath Passage and have remained ever since.

157. A return to open-air bathing was made in 1934 with the opening of Surbiton Lagoon in Raeburn Avenue. It closed in 1979 and the site is now occupied by housing and a park.

A Shopping Town

SHRUBSOLE'S

Kingston has a long shopping history – borough deeds mention shops at least as early as 1315. For the next 500 years they were small, specialist places, trading in or near the Market Place. Then came the railways, which brought an influx of new, moneyed residents who were unimpressed by Kingston's plain little shops, and preferred to go by train to the enticing London emporia. Reluctantly, Kingston began refurbishing its shopping image, often by tacking a showy new frontage to an existing old building. Many such examples survive in Thames Street, Market Place and High Street, the premier shopping streets until the arrival of tramcars. The leader of this retail shopping revolution was Shrubsole's, founded in Kingston Market Place by a Mr Clarkson in 1760. Under

158. (Below) George Bennett's linen drapery at 28 High Street boasted members of the Royal Family among its customers – hence the Royal Arms over the door. The future Queen Mary bought linen here before her wedding to the future George V. The shop is here decorated for the Jubilee of 1897.

159. (Right) This was a brazier's shop and home in 1570. Later to be no. 14 Market Place, it was acquired by Boot's, and is now part of Next.

160. Shrubsole's old shop in Market Place in 1897, when owned by Joseph Hide. The flags mark Queen Victoria's Diamond Jubilee

161. The famous 'Tudor' facade applied by Boot's to its store at nos. 15 and 16 Market Place. The carvings illustrate aspects of Kingston's history.

162. Nuthall's provisions department in 1904. This was the 'Fortnum & Mason' of Kingston, catering for the most affluent of Kingston's residents.

various names and owners, it remained there until 1986 as the oldest retail business in Kingston, and one of the oldest in Britain.

It was already a store of the highest social standing, favoured with the custom of Queen Victoria and her family, when brothers John and Henry Shrubsole enlarged and reorganised it on London department store lines in 1866. Four years later they engaged Decimus Burton, architect of the triumphal arch at Hyde Park Corner, to design an elegant frontage described by the *Surrey Comet* as "a style never before attempted in this town... few houses of business in town or country could be found to surpass it." In 1873 the store was bought by Joseph Hide and continued under his name until 1977, when it was bought by the House of Fraser.

BENTALLS

But Kingston's most famous retailing achievement was – and is – Bentalls. In 1867 Frank Bentall acquired a small drapery shop at 31 Clarence Street. He was 24, in love, and hoped that by setting up in business he would win the approval of his prospective father-in-law. His chances looked slim. His little shop had been a drapery for at least the previous three decades, but had never made much money for its previous owner, James Hatt.

One reason was that Clarence Street was an unfashionable thoroughfare, consisting mainly of ancient shops and cottages and a few old inns. Kingston's prime shopping areas were the Market Place and Thames Street, and had been since medieval times. Another factor was that there were no fewer than 25 drapers competing for custom in the town centre.

James Hatt had been sure that Clarence Street's day would come because it was a through route to King-

163. *Frank Bentall's shop in Clarence Street in 1912.*

164. *Wood Street, seen here in the 1890s, looking south from the junction with Skerne Road, was an old-world thoroughfare until the early twentieth century. Now, all the left side is covered by Bentalls store and the Bentalls Centre, and most of the right side by Bentalls multi-storey car park, offices and the John Lewis complex.*

165. Bentalls beautiful Tudor Restaurant in the 1930s.

166. Bentalls Corner, just before demolition and rebuilding in 1935.

167. Bentalls in Wood Street/Clarence Street, as rebuilt by Aston Webb in 1935. The store's facade was inspired by the William & Mary wing of Hampton Court Palace. It was preserved in a brilliant piece of engineering when the store was demolished in 1990.

ston Bridge. He was right. But it happened too late for him, and it was eventually Frank Bentall who reaped the benefit. Frank's first week's gross takings were about £70, but by the end of the first year they had risen to an average of £200. It was then he and later his son, Leonard, began the gradual expansion that was eventually to make Bentalls the largest privately owned store in Europe until it went public in 1946.

POST-WAR CHANGES

Kingston's post-war shopping development began with the building of the Eden Walk shopping complex and multi-storey car park, built in three stages (1964-66, 1977-79 and 1985). This dramatically changed the townscape of Eden Street and Union Street, and paved the way for Kingston's pre-eminence as a shopping centre. In 1987 Bentalls teamed with Norwich Union to develop the Bentall Centre. This, completed in 1992, is the largest retail scheme ever carried out in Kingston. It involved demolishing Bentalls premises and replacing them with a new department store linked to a four-floor shopping mall. The only surviving part of the old store is its world-renowned Wood Street frontage, modelled by architect Aston Webb on the William and Mary wing of Hampton Court Palace.

While the Bentall Centre was under construction, a new John Lewis department store was being built immediately opposite, on the Horsefair. It opened in 1990, and its award-winning design by Ahrends Burton & Koralek had to incorporate part of the relief road, which runs through the site. Meanwhile Marks & Spencer had embarked on a programme which, when completed in 1995, made the Kingston branch one of the top four in Britain.

By 1997 these and other initiatives had given Kingston 3.5 million square feet of retail space, making it the largest shopping centre in the South-East outside central London, and the seventh largest in the UK.

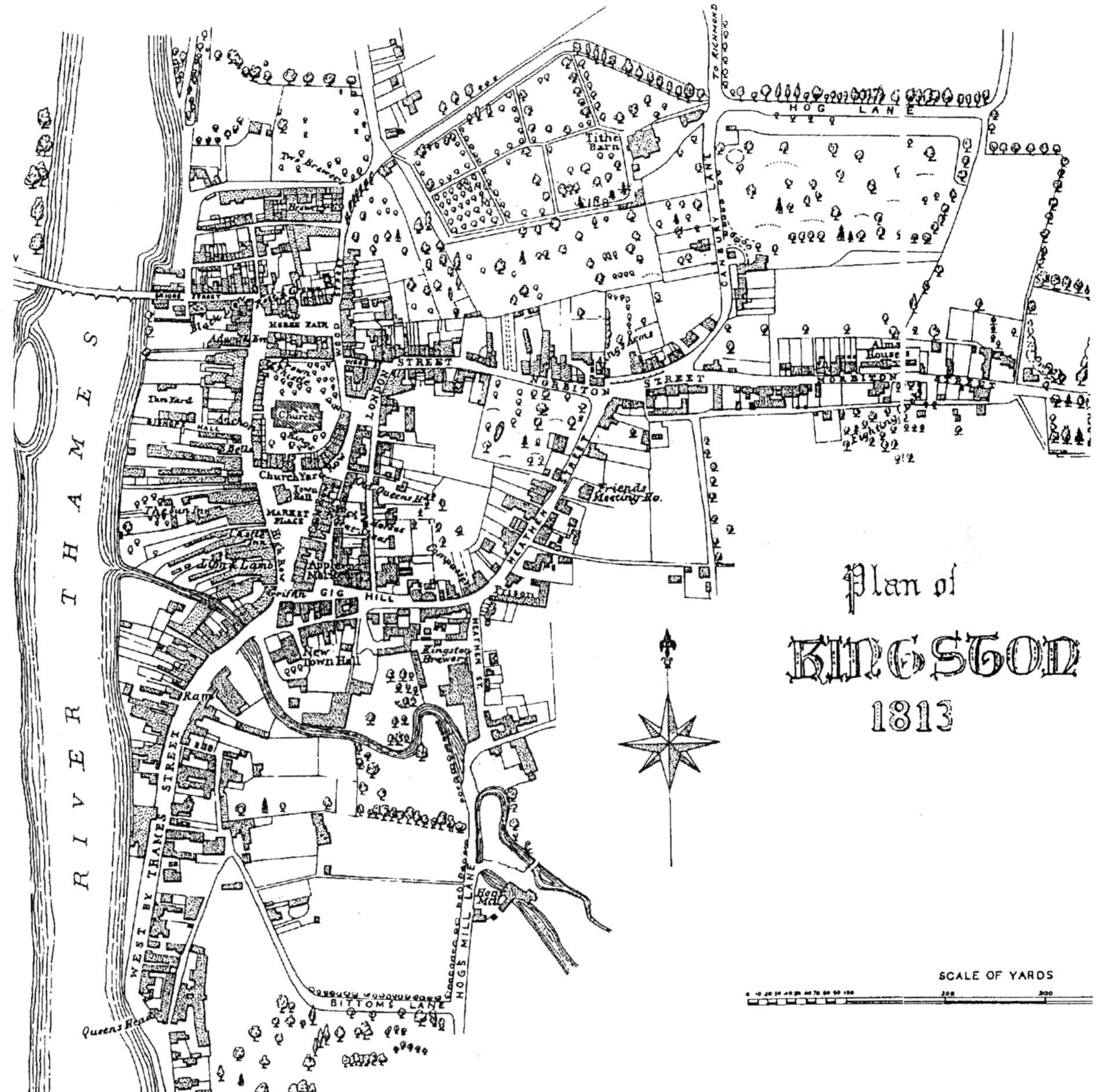

168. *Well before Suburbia – Kingston in 1813. This plan by Thomas Hornor shows Kingston as it looked for centuries, before the enclosure of commons, the re-siting of Kingston Bridge, and the arrival of railways.*

The Growth of Suburbia

The opening of the Kingston By-pass in 1927 did more than divert traffic from the town centre. It led to the disappearance of most of the farms in the area, and their replacement by miles of semi-detached suburbia

The road, designed by county surveyor W.P. Robinson, was longer, costlier and more devious than the original route planned before the First World War. For Surrey County Council failed to 'freeze' the land they needed, and in the intervening years so much building took place that diversions had to be made.

The By-pass, begun in 1924, carved through virgin countryside and had a particular impact on Tolworth, which in 1927 was scarcely more than a hamlet. Four years later, farms and arable land had been replaced by 6.5 miles of streets, 57 shops, 1,300 houses and 6,250 residents.

That was just the beginning. In February 1931 a further 308 houses were being erected, while work was about to start on 323 more. Sites had been acquired for three churches and a large school, while Surbiton District Council was planning an open-air swimming bath "for the requirements of cleanliness". This materialised as Surbiton Lagoon.

Nine building firms had stakes in land by the by-pass, and engaged in a construction race that local families likened to a gold rush. Land was devoured with almost wanton speed in a building stampede to put up houses 'on spec'. Most were small, priced between £600 and £1,00. But they were set in wide and pleasant streets; and estate agents could still, with some truth, extol the "light and airy country atmosphere".

Previously the fields of the Tolworth Lodge, Tolworth Court, Smith's and Berrylands farms had formed unbroken farmland from what became the by-pass at Tolworth to Surbiton Hill and the future Elmbridge Avenue. After the by-pass opening, Tolworth Broadway was carved through the rich arable and grazing fields of Tolworth Lodge, while the farmhouse itself was replaced by a service station at the Broadway/Ewell Road junction. Tolworth Girls' School and the adjoining recreation centre were built on the fields of Fuller's Farm. Smith's Farm gave way to Elgar Avenue and other residential roads. Berrylands Farm disappeared beneath Manor Drive, Manor Crescent and other developments.

A 'Tudor' home was what many people longed for, giving the illusion of old-world rurality in a relentlessly urban world. The most celebrated of Kingston's new developments was the Tudor Estate, opened in November 1933 on what had been orchard and nursery land between Richmond Road and Richmond Park. Each of the hundreds of houses on the estate boasted timbering, gabling and leaded windows, and the first hundred were sold in only six weeks. Prices started at £675 freehold with repayments at a weekly 17s 4d. It was, said G.T. Crouch, the builder, "perfect for the man on £4 10s. a week." The most expensive cost £955, repayable at 25s 7d per week, which Crouch declared to be for a man "with a position in the City, bringing home a steady salary of £7 a week."

169 & 170. Two houses on the Tudor Estate. Above is 'The Kingston', selling for £675, and below 'The Latchmere' model for £955.

In 1932, the Fitzgeorge family sold its Coombe Estate to Higgs & Hill. The deal involved more than 700 acres with two miles of frontage to Kingston By-pass and extensive frontages to Coombe Lane. Farms, meadows, woods and fine gardens gave way to a network of roads, including Burghley and Neville Avenues, Cromford and Bakewell Ways, the Darley, Buxton and High Drives, and Dickerage, Albion and Crown Roads.

Modern Pleasures

Kingston's first cinema opened on 22 August, 1908 at St James's Hall in St James's Road. Here Bert Carn introduced movies with admission prices ranging from 1½p to 7½p. The *Surrey Comet* commented: "The novelty of bioscope pictures being enhanced by the accompanying gramophone selections drew a large audience." In 1913 Castleton Knight leased the hall and converted it into the Kingston Coliseum, "The premier picture theatre. The house of laughter, tears and thrills." The First World War, plus fierce competition, finished the Coliseum in 1916. The building then became the furniture depository of Smithers & Sons until 1938, when it was acquired by the cycle firm Owen Ltd. They occupied it, with a cafe in the basement, until it was sold for redevelopment in 1961. The Unilever complex now covers the site.

Kingston Picture Theatre opened on the corner of Cromwell Road in 1910 on part of the former parkland of Canbury Lodge. It was owned by Surrey and Sussex Picture Palaces of Kingston Hill, and was designed by Walter Phillips to seat 400. An advance advertisement promised "the projecting apparatus will be the most scientifically that money can purchase; the scratched, worn-out, badly focussed, jerky picture will find no place." The theatre eventually evolved into Studio 7, which closed in 1983.

Kingston's first purpose-built cinema was the Cinem Palace, built at the corner of Richmond Road and Canbury Park Road in 1909 by James Watt. He called it "a palace of dreams", which extended to free tea and biscuits in the interval. Watt demolished it in 1932 and replaced it with the Regal, which seated 3,000 and cost £150,000. It took 200 men more than a year to build this sumptuous cinema, designed by Robert Cromie in soft-toned brick contrasting with

171. The first cinema in Kingston, a converted hall, became the Coliseum. It was closed in 1916 in the face of more sophisticated opposition, and became a furniture store of Smithers & Sons.

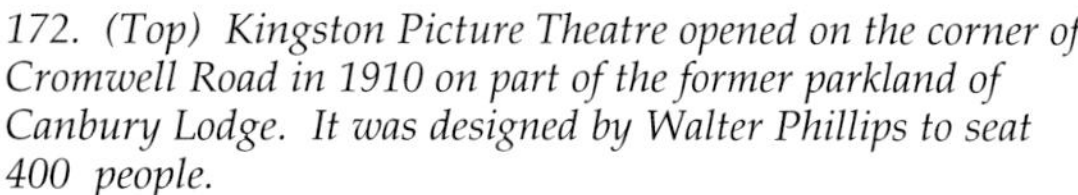

172. (Top) Kingston Picture Theatre opened on the corner of Cromwell Road in 1910 on part of the former parkland of Canbury Lodge. It was designed by Walter Phillips to seat 400 people.

173. (Bottom left) The Cinem Palace, the first purpose-built cinema in Kingston, at the corner of Richmond Road and Canbury Park Road in 1909.

174. (Right) The Regal, designed by Robert Cromie.

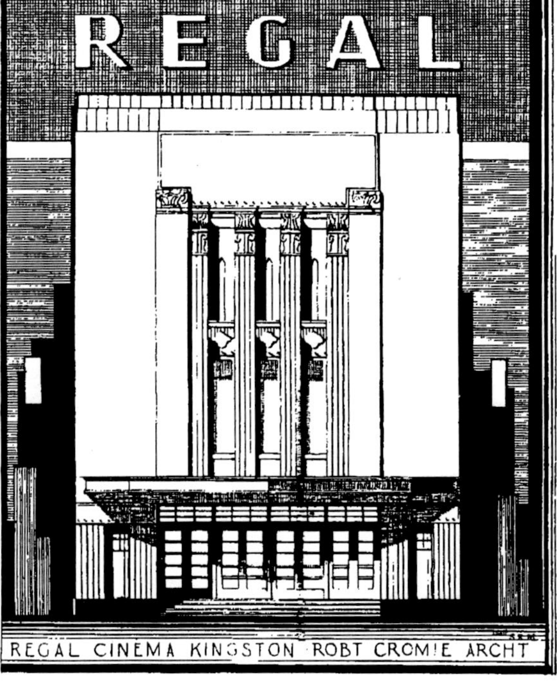

175. (Left) The Odeon, Kingston High Street.

176. (Below) The Elite cinema at the junction of London Road and Clarence Street, said to be one of the most beautiful picture houses ever built. It is seen here shortly before its demolition in 1954.

177. (Above) The site of the Elite cinema, by C. Bigot in 1830.

178. The Royal County Theatre in Fife Road, c.1908.

white carved and fluted stonework. The Regal Cafe opened at 11am each day, with tea dances from 4pm to 6pm, and dancing each evening from 8 to 10.30pm. The building was closed as a cinema in 1976 and has been a bingo hall ever since.

Kingston's place in cinema history is not only as the birthplace of Eadweard Muybridge, the photographer who pioneered moving pictures, but as one of the three places chosen to launch the great Odeon circuit. This was conceived by a former scrap metal dealer called Oscar Deutsch, who chose the name Odeon because the first two letters of the word formed his initials. When he launched the Odeon organisation in 1933, he directed that work in Kingston should begin immediately. Thus the Odeon in Kingston High Street opened that same year. Two more opened in Tolworth and Surbiton a few months later, and in 1938 another at Shannon's Corner, New Malden. Deutsch created some 350 cinemas before his death in 1941.

The Kingston Odeon closed in 1967, but reopened the following month as a bingo club. It was demolished in 1988 for development that never materialised. By coincidence, the Kingston Odeon adjoined Muybridge's birthplace, which is seen on the left in Illustration 175.

There were two theatres in Kingston. The Kingston Empire was built in 1910. Its famous dome, pictured in Illustration 179 being put into place, was only the second in Britain to be illuminated, the first being that of the London Coliseum. Every British variety artist of note played here until the theatre closed in 1955. Then the building was converted into a shop. In 1997 it became a pub.

The Royal County Theatre opened in Fife Road in 1897. It seated 1,300, had a large orchestra pit, and mounted productions of variety, farce and grand opera. It closed in 1912, defeated by the advent of easier transport to the West End, and competition from cinema. The building became the Super Cinema in 1917, and in 1929 the first cinema in Kingston to show 'talkies', when it screeened *The Singing Fool* on 10 July. In 1949 it was gutted by fire.

Another well-known pleasure in Kingston was a visit to Nuthall's restaurants, banquetting rooms and pleasure gardens in Thames Street, opened in 1902. One of the most elegant social venues in Surrey, it was designed by Kingston architects Carter & Ashworth with a splendid street frontage, part of which survives. It closed in 1933, a victim of the Depression, and was bought by British Home Stores. A branch of Milletts now occupies the site.

179. Kingston Empire's famous dome being put into place on the almost complete theatre in 1910. The dome was only the second in Britain to be illuminated (the first being the London Coliseum).

180. The interior of Nuthall's Rosebery Room in Thames Street, one of the most elegant social venues in Surrey. Nuthall's closed in 1933, a victim of the Depression. Part of the street frontage survives.

181. *'Tom' Sopwith.*

Kingston in the Air

Kingston played a key role in the birth of the British aircraft industry. In 1912 Thomas Octave Murdoch (TOM) Sopwith founded his Sopwith Aviation Co. in a former Kingston roller skating rink, and since then Britain's defence forces have never been without a Kingston-designed aircraft in front-line service.

Less well-known is that another aviation pioneer was designing and making aircraft in Kingston years before Sopwith. He was Thomas Wigston Kingslake Clarke, who in 1903 set up business as Britain's first aeronautical consulting engineer. His base was Crown Works at 22 Kingston High Street, where he produced craft advertised as 'man-carrying gliders' and 'man-carrying aeroplanes' priced from £40 and £400 respectively. Little is known of the man-carrying aeroplanes ("framework, engines, surfaces, propellers and spare parts to customers own requirements"), but Clarke was widely acclaimed for his biplane gliders, one of which had a wing span of 39 feet, and introduced the use of silver spruce and dope to the aviation industry. Another glider, built in 1909 for Alec Ogilvie, made record quarter-mile glides. Clarke's Kingston works also produced the first commercially available model aeroplane made in

182. *Kingston Skating Rink in Canbury Park Road, where Sopwith established his aviation company.*

183. (Top) Thomas Clarke takes to the air in his 'man-carrying glider'.

184. The Sopwith factory at Canbury Park Road.

Britain. Known as the 'Clarke Flyer', it went on sale for Christmas 1907 in five different sizes, and was the first British model plane capable of long flights.

Though Clarke became well known for his propellers (one held the world record for efficiency), and had a full order book for scale models and model making equipment, his company never made a profit. He was forced to close it in 1912 – ironically, the same year Tom Sopwith was installing his new firm in the skating rink at 1 Canbury Park Road.

Sopwith began with a workforce of seven. Five years later, due to the First World War, it had risen to 3,500. Sopwith's first Kingston plane was the Tabloid, made in great secrecy to a design chalked out on the old rink's wooden floors. It achieved speeds of more than 90 mph, making it the world's fastest aeroplane. It was also the forerunner of all the single-seat aircraft of the First World War, and devastated the airship sheds at Dusseldorf and Cologne. Another Sopwith aircraft, the Camel, was said to have shot down the legendary Red Baron.

As demand for fighter planes increased, the old rink became inadequate. Sopwith then bought up several nearby shops and cottages, and replaced them with a hurriedly built factory. Here, some of the greatest developments in the history of aviation took place until 1962, when the company transferred to Richmond Road.

The industrial history of this 36-acre site had begun in 1917 with the launch of the National Factory Scheme,

—SOPWITH AVIATION C° L^TD KINGSTON.—
—HAM WORKS. DEC. 1918.—
—S.704.—

185. *Salamanders in production at the Richmond Road works in 1918.*

186. *A 1976 view of Hawker's works in Richmond Road. It shows how the impressive 1950s frontage was pinned to the huge factory building constructed in 1918. The works were demolished in 1992, and the site is now a large housing estate.*

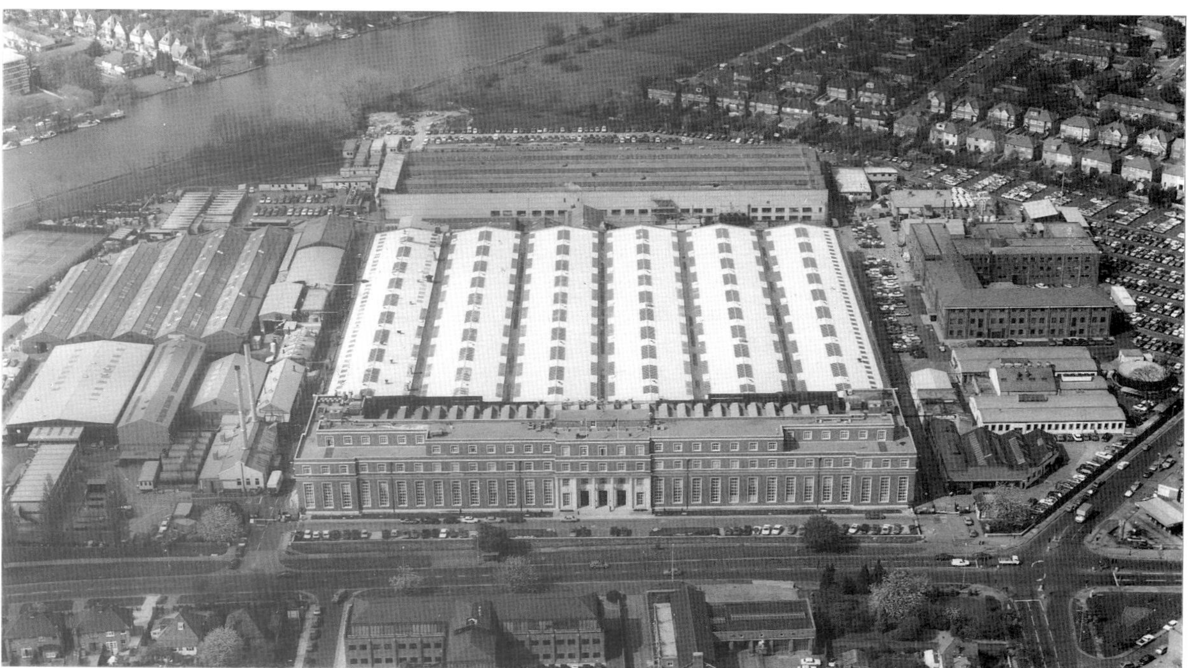

187. Another air pioneer with local links was Jim Mollison, who spent his last lonely years running the Carisbrooke Hotel in St Philip's Road, Surbiton, and died forgotten in 1959. Yet he had been one of the greatest of all the long-distance solo pilots, and in 1932 married the famous aviatrix, Amy Johnson – they are pictured above. In 1933 the pair made the first direct, non-stop flight from Britain to the USA.

under which the Government paid for premises, and manufacturers managed them. Four such factories were planned in Kingston, but only the Richmond Road site was completed. Thus it was known throughout the First World War as Aircraft Factory Number 1. Sopwith was initially in favour of the scheme, then had misgivings. He was right, because the exercise proved an expensive failure.

Fortunately he had opted out, so could make an independent bid for the new factory. He was offered a new lease and took it. This initial building, where the first plane was completed on 1 June, 1918, was an enormous shed in the centre of the site, with ancillary buildings to the north and south. By 1918 Sopwith was producing ninety planes a week here, mainly Snipes and Salamanders.

The Armistice led to a slump in the aircraft industry and Sopwith Aviation was wound up on 15 November, 1920. But on the same day it was replaced by H. G. Hawker Engineering. The new company was named after Sopwith's brilliant young test pilot, Harry Hawker, who was tragically killed the following year while practising for the Aerial Derby.

The Richmond Road factory was then leased to Leyland Motors. When that lease expired in 1948, the Hawker Company took the site and resumed aircraft production there, although the design and administration offices, and the machine shops, remained in Canbury Park Road for several more years.

The company that began as Sopwith Aviation took on various names over the years. From 1920 to 1933 it was H.G. Hawker Engineering; from 1933 to 1963 it was Hawker Aircraft; from 1963 to 1977 it was part of Hawker Siddeley Aviation and from 1977 it became part of British Aerospace.

Since the beginning of flight, there has been no aerial campaign involving the UK in which a Kingston aircraft has not been involved. First World War examples include the Camel, Pup, Tabloid and One and a Half Strutter. Second World War aircraft included the Hurricane, Tempest and Typhoon. In the Korean war there was the Sea Fury, in the Falklands the Sea Harrier and Harrier, and in the Gulf War the Harrier again, as part of the US Marine Corps.

In all, more than 44,000 aircraft were produced in Kingston until 1992. That year saw the closure of British Aerospace and the end of eighty years of aircraft design and manufacture in the Royal borough. The social and economic shockwaves are still reverberating. For this was Kingston's biggest employer, and around 40,000 people had jobs there during its eight decades. Yet the whole, vast enterprise originated for no better reason than that a rich man's son called Thomas Sopwith got a craze for flying in 1910.

Modern Kingston

A HOUSE FAMINE

No-one noticed the German plane that flew high over Kingston on 12 August 1940, its hidden cameras taking photographs of potential targets. As a result, Kingston suffered more wartime raids than might have been expected; for the targets pinpointed by the Luftwaffe included the Hawker aircraft factory, the gasworks and the sewage and waterworks. In the event, all escaped unscathed, save for damage to part of Hawker's factory in Canbury Park Road. But there were more than thirty bombing raids, which killed and injured about a thousand people in Kingston, Surbiton and New Malden, and damaged or destroyed more than a thousand properties.

Thus homelessness was the hottest single issue after the war ended in 1945. Bombs, plus the return of thousands of service personnel, had led to such a desperate housing famine that many buildings were requisitioned, temporary huts and pre-fabs were hastily put up, and it was commonplace to find twelve or more people sharing a three-bedroomed house.

Kingston Council, after fruitless attempts to annexe land in neighbouring boroughs, embarked on an ambitious home-building programme. It included Elm House, built in Elm Road as the council's first apartment block; and Cambridge Gardens, the largest and best quality block of council flats in Surrey when it opened in 1949. The latter was a notable victory over Whitehall, for the goverment wanted the site of the former Royal Cambridge Asylum for Soldiers' Widows preserved as an open space. Kingston stubbornly refused to take no for an answer, and in 1946 prised permission to demolish the asylum and build 160 high-quality flats. In return, it promised to create an open space on the opposite side of Cambridge Road. That promise was not kept. Today the land opposite is covered by Cambridge Road Estate, Kingston's first, and certainly last, venture into high-rise housing. The site had previously been covered by streets of Victorian cottages, shops and pubs. It took a decade of planning, land acquisition, demolition and construction before the scheme was finally completed in 1973. The result was 1,322 dwellings, housing close on 3,000 people at a cost of £2.75 million. These homes were sorely needed in a borough where, because of Richmond Park and the river, building land has always been limited. But the 17-storey tower blocks have been a controversial topic ever since.

CHANGE IN THE CENTRE

Since the war, much of central Kingston has been altered beyond recognition by commercial development. Massive changes began in 1964 with Eden Walk Stage I. In the 1970s came Eden Walk II plus the total redevelopment of Brook Street to make way for the huge Lever complex on one side, and government offices on the other. The same decade brought startling changes to Fairfield West, where a hugely controversial block replaced small shops and cottages. The loss of familiar old landmarks reached its peak in the 80s, when a short stroll in any direction brought one to building projects that by 1984 had increased Kingston's office space by more than 80%. There was more to come, notably the 150,000 square feet in Kingsgate House, completed in Wood Street in 1986 as the largest office development ever seen in Kingston.

A potent symbol of the economic changes that have swept post-war Kingston is the replacement of many local industries by residential development. A prime example is in Richmond Road, where hundreds of homes have been built on the former site of British Aerospace, which closed in 1992. Houses have replaced the Vine Products works in Villiers Road, which closed in 1989. A major house-building programme has begun on the site of Kingston Power Station, which closed in 1980, while homes, shops and leisure facilities are planned for the site of Kingston Gasworks. Even the former goods yards and coal wharves adjacent to Kingston station have been given over to apartment blocks.

This decline of Kingston as a manufacturing centre has led to much change in employment. In 1981 some 22% of the local workforce was engaged in manufacturing. This had fallen to 15% in 1991, and to under 7.4% by 1994.

So much change, concentrated in such a short time, has been hard to take. But on the whole Kingstonians have come to terms with it and are happy that in an age when out-of-town malls are ruining many an urban economy, Kingston has bucked the trend.

All that change has, ironically, boosted interest in conservation and in the past. In 1962 the Kingston Society was formed by a group of architects to encourage high standards of architecture, to stimulate interest in the beauty, history and character of the town, and to encourage preservation and improvement of features. When, in 1963, it was proposed that Kingston should have a ring road, part of which would run along the riverside, the Society was an important influence in getting the road plans altered, and achieving the pedestrianisation of Market Place and Clarence Street. Since then it has been instrumental in saving various historic buildings

Kingston Museum has also been regenerated. It began, together with an art gallery, in 1904 as an

188. The opening of Kingston Library by Andrew Carnegie in 1903 – he is standing next to the mayoress, Mrs Thomas Lyne, centre. The other people are aldermen, councillors and officers.

adjunct of the free library built in Fairfield after a generous donation from the philanthropist, Andrew Carnegie. The building was designed by Alfred Cox in English Renaissance style. In 1992 the Museum closed for a £300,000 refurbishment and reopened two years later with a modernised art gallery and permanent displays showing the history of Kingston up to Saxon times. Thanks to a National Lottery grant of nearly £105,000, the transformation was completed in 1997 with the addition of 'Town of Kings', a brilliant display that takes Kingston's history up to the present. This, together with the Heritage Service for local history research at the North Kingston Centre in Richmond Road, has made the Museum a great educational asset.

Much of Kingston's past is a mystery that has lain hidden below ground for centuries. Not until the 1960s, when key sites were being cleared, could archaeology enthusiasts seize the chance to try unearthing answers before developers moved in.

A major find emerged in 1968 – still known in local history circles as Jackpot Year – when a volunteer team found part of a fourteenth-century pottery kiln behind 70/72 Eden Street.

Medieval Kingston was already known to have supplied the royal household and others with pottery and tableware; but it was assumed to have been made elsewhere, with Kingston serving only as a trading channel. The unearthing of the kiln, with more than half a ton of pottery, proved the town had also been a pottery manufacturing centre for Surrey white ware. The rest of the kiln, together with three more, was discovered in 1995 on the site now covered by C & A.

189. Kingston Museum and Library in 1904. The Museum is in the foreground.

In 1969 the volunteer diggers, led by Marion Shipley of Kingston Museum, formed Kingston upon Thames Archaeological Society, choosing as its emblem a king's head from a fourteenth-century Surrey whiteware jug. Since then the society has taken part in many digs, uncovering much new evidence about this unique town.

Further Reading

Anderson, A: *History and antiquities of the ancient town of Kingston Upon Thames* (1818).

Aubrey, J: *The natural History and Antiquities of the County of Surrey* (1718).

Ayliffe, G.W: *Old Kingston: Recollections of an Octogenarian* (1914).

Bellars, Margaret: *Kingston Then and Now* (1977).

Bentall, Rowan: My Store of Memories (1974).

Besse, J: A Collection of the Suffering of the People called Quakers (1753).

Biden, W.D: *The History of Antiquities of Kingston Upon Thames* (1852).

Blackmore, L.K: *A Biography of Harry Hawker* (1993).

Brayley and Britton: *History of Surrey*, Vol. 2 (1850).

Broome, H: *Kingston Union: The Beginning and the End* (1930).

Bryan, W.C: *Bygone Memories of Kingston and Norbiton* (1932).

Butters, Shaan: *Kingston Past* (1995).

A House of Prayer. The History of St Peter's Church, Norbiton (1992).

Clarke, N.J: *Adolf Hitler's Home Counties Holiday Snaps* (1996).

Clay, R.M: *The Medieval Hospitals of England* (1909).

Daley, Anne: *Kingston Upon Thames Apprentices 1569-1713* (1974).

Dendy, Marshall C.F: *History of the Southern Railway* (1963).

Finny, W.E. St L: *Medieval Games and Gatherings at Kingston Upon Thames* (1936).

The Church of the Saxon Coronations at Kingston (1943).

The Borough of Kingston Ancient and Modern (1902).

Fozard, J: *Sydney Camm and the Hurricane* (1991).

Godden, J.S: *British Aerospace Presents 75 years of Aviation in Kingston* (1988).

Hardman, W. ed. S.M. Ellis: *The Hardman Papers* (1930).

Harley, R.J: *Kingston and Wimbledon Tramways* (1955).

Harper, C: *The Portsmouth Road* (revised edn 1923).

Heales, A: *The Early History of the Church of Kingston Upon Thames* (1883).

Hillier, J: *Old Surrey Water Mills*

Kelly's Directories

Kingston Grammar School: *Quatercentenary booklet* (1961).

Kingston and Surbiton Times (1882-1900).

Kingston Upon Thames and Surbiton, HIstory, Trade and Attractions in 1891 (reprint 1979).

Leeson, D. and Woodriffe, B: *How Electricity came to Kingston* (1980).

Leland, John: *Itinerary of England and Wales* (2nd edn 1744).

Leyland Motor Corporation. *Leyland: Seventy Years of Progress* (1966).

Lown, S. and Panizzo, P: *A Fair and High Locality* (1996).

Lysons, Daniel: *Environs of London* (1792).

McCormack, Anne: *Royal Kingston* (1988).

Kingston Upon Thames, A Pictorial History (1989).

Merryweather, F.S: *Half a Century of Kingston History* (1881).

Morris, John ed: *Domesday Book – Surrey* (1975).

Penn, J, Field, D. and Seargentson, D: 'Evidence of Neolithic Occupation in Kingston: Excavations at Eden Walk.' *Surrey Archaeological Collections* Vol. 75 (1984).

Perkins, H.H: *Bentalls, Over 80 years of progressive achievement 1867-1951.*

Phillipson's Directory

Pink, J.R: *The Excise Officers and their Duties in an English Market Town* (1995).

Pulford, J.S.L: *The first Kingston Quakers.*

Richardson, R.W.C: *Surbiton: Thirty-two years of Local Self Government, 1885-1997* (1888).

Robinson's Railway Directory.

Robinson, D: *Craftsman's Art and Music's Measure* (1988).

Roots, George: *Charters of Kingston upon Thames*(1797).

Sampson, June: *All Change: Kingston, Surbiton and New Malden in the 19th Century* (1985).

The Story of Kingston (1972).

Kingston and Surbiton Old and New.

Savage, J.H: *Non-Conformity in Kingston* (1920)

Smeeton, C.D: *The London United Tramways*, Vol. 1: 'Origins to 1912' (1994).

Smiths Industries: *K.L.G: From Cars to Concorde* (1989).

Statham, R: *Surbiton Past* (1996).

Stenton, F.M: *Anglo Saxon England* (1971).

Sturney, A.C: *The Story of Kingston Congregational Churches.*

Surrey Comet (1854-1997).

Wakeford, Joan: *Kingston's Past Rediscovered* (1990).

White, H.P: *A Regional History of the Railways of Great Britain.*

Whitelocke, D: *English Historical Documents 500-1042* (1955).

Wilkinson, B: *The Coronation's History* (1953).

Young, Harry: *The church in the Market Place – The Story of Kingston's Baptist Church* (1990).

INDEX

Asterisks denote illustrations